The Free Peasantry
of the
Northern Danelaw

The Free Peasantry
of the
Northern Danelaw

F. M. STENTON

OXFORD

AT THE CLARENDON PRESS

1969

Oxford University Press, Ely House, London W. 1

GLASGOW NEW YORK TORONTO MELBOURNE WELLINGTON
CAPE TOWN SALISBURY IBADAN NAIROBI LUSAKA ADDIS ABABA
BOMBAY CALCUTTA MADRAS KARACHI LAHORE DACCA
KUALA LUMPUR SINGAPORE HONG KONG TOKYO

*Originally published in the
Bulletin de la Société Royale Des Lettres
de Lund 1925-6*

PRINTED IN GREAT BRITAIN

Contents

Introductory Note

THIS book gives the substance of a lecture delivered at
Lund, Sweden, at the invitation of the Royal Society of
Letters of Lund and is here reprinted with the gracious
permission of the Society. It is based on a large number of
charters collected over many years and was first printed in
the *Bulletin de la Société Royale des Lettres de Lund*, 1925–6. In
preparing it for publication I have corrected a few slips and
tried to indicate where a few of the charters which have
been reprinted since 1926 have appeared. I have also made
an Index.

DORIS MARY STENTON

The Free Peasantry of the Northern Danelaw[1]

THE most distinctive feature of the early medieval economy of the part of England known as the Danelaw is the great body of peasants who individually enjoyed personal independence. Such peasants perhaps occur in greatest number in East Anglia, but the medieval society of this region has not yet been discussed in sufficient detail to show the exact significance of their presence. In Yorkshire, again, there is evidence of a considerable free population on the eve of the Conquest, but the great devastation of this shire carried through by William I in 1069 destroyed its prosperity, and broke the course of its agrarian development. Between East Anglia and Yorkshire, in the region known before the Norman Conquest as the territory of the Five Boroughs, a free population established long before the reign of William I continued in possession of its ancient rights and liberties throughout the whole of the Middle Ages. It is with this region that the present study is concerned.[2]

The Five Boroughs which gave name to the region were

[1] First printed in *Bulletin de la société royale des lettres de Lund*, 1925–6.
[2] Upon the early material for the agrarian history of the Danelaw I would refer to the introduction to my *Danelaw Charters* (British Academy) pp. xiv–xix. This book only included original documents of the twelfth century. Texts preserved in cartularies fell outside its scope.

Lincoln, Nottingham, Derby, Leicester, and Stamford. The first four of them are still the county towns of modern shires. There has been remarkably little change in their administrative geography since the date of the Domesday survey. There has been no material change in the boundaries of the several counties since 1086. In Lincolnshire and Nottinghamshire the smaller units of local government, the wapentakes, underwent little alteration thenceforward. In Leicestershire, one of the four wapentakes which existed in 1086, was divided into two, apparently in the twelfth century, but no further alteration of consequence was made. It is only in Derbyshire that there was any serious remodelling of the wapentakes, and even there the main line of the ancient divisions can still be recovered. With these exceptions, any map of the counties which includes the boundaries of wapentakes may be trusted to represent with substantial accuracy their outlines in 1086.[1]

For many centuries there was singularly little change in what may be called the feudal geography of the region, in the distribution of estates and in their general character. This is the more remarkable in that the medieval distribution of land in the northern Danelaw was of very ancient

[1] No one has yet attempted a detailed topographical investigation of the wapentakes and hundreds of England. For the Danelaw, Morden's maps, as they appear, for example, in the 1695 (folio) edition of Camden's *Britannia*, are useful. For Lincolnshire, the map given by Canon Foster in his edition of the Lincolnshire Domesday (*Lincoln Record Society*, vol. 19) is definitive. The boundaries of the Leicestershire wapentakes are indicated in the Domesday map contained in the *Victoria History of Leicestershire* vol. i. *See* O.S. Anderson's *English Hundred-Names*, Lund, 1934 and 1939.

origin and differed markedly from the much more regular
and uniform manorial economy which prevailed in the
south.[1] In Lincolnshire and Nottinghamshire the typical
form of estate prevalent in 1066 consisted of a lord's house,
the *manerium* of Domesday, with a home farm attached to
it, with unfree peasants, the *villani* and *bordarii* of Domesday,
living in the same village, and, if later evidence may be
followed, assisting in the cultivation of the lord's land.
Thus far, the Danelaw economy only followed lines of
development common to all England. The distinctive
feature of the Danelaw system was the association of the
villani and *bordarii* with a third class of men, known in
Domesday under the name of *sochemanni*, of whose personal
freedom there can be no question. Domesday Book tells
little of their status and services, and it is only recently
that later material has been used to illustrate their position.
But it is now becoming clear that the Danelaw 'sokeman',
though bound to his lord by the tie of homage and by such
payments and services as resulted by custom therefrom,
was yet in a real sense his own master. He had his own
recognized place in the courts of wapentake and shire. He
could alienate his land or any portion of it by gift, sale, or

[1] In a series of articles published in the *Victoria Histories of Nottinghamshire, Derbyshire, and Leicestershire*, I have attempted to indicate the points
of agrarian interest brought out by the Domesday descriptions of these
shires. The series is continued by the introduction to the Domesday
survey of Lincolnshire published by the Lincoln Record Society. A more
technical account of the manorial economy of the region as a whole is
contained in my essay *Types of Manorial Structure in the Northern Danelaw*
(Oxford Studies in Social and Legal History, vol. ii, pp. 1–96).

exchange. He paid his taxes, such as the Danegeld or the sheriff's aid, directly to the officers of the king or the sheriff. Above all, he was usually free from the villein's duty of working two or more days each week on his lord's land.[1] He was therefore free from the compulsion of manorial discipline. No doubt, on many estates the sokeman was expected to help his lord by supplying labour at those seasons of the year when work was heaviest, such as haytime and harvest. But there was nothing derogatory in service of this kind, nor did it in any way detract from the sokeman's personal independence.

The distribution of this great class of sokemen over the Danelaw has not yet received the attention which it deserves. In particular, the relative numbers of sokemen on the one hand and *villani* and *bordarii* on the other, according to the enumeration of these classes in Domesday Book, have never yet been worked out in detail, wapentake by wapentake. The tables which follow represent the result of an analysis of the Domesday surveys of the Danelaw shires which has occupied the present writer intermittently for many years.[2] Absolute accuracy cannot indeed be claimed

[1] The only example of week work due from sokemen which I have noticed in early records occurs in the *Liber Niger* of Peterborough (1125) where 29 sokemen at Scotter in Lincolnshire appear as owing one day's work each week, and two days a week throughout August.

[2] I wish to acknowledge the great help I have received in the analysis of the Lincolnshire figures from my colleague Mr. S. A. Peyton, Librarian of the University of Reading. The second volume of the edition of the Lincolnshire Domesday to be published by the Lincoln Record Society will consist of a detailed analysis of the Survey of this county, village by village, by Canon T. Longley. [This volume has never been completed.]

for these figures. Some entries in Domesday are ambiguous. In some cases it is possible that a village has been wrongly identified, and referred to a wrong wapentake. But on the whole it is probable that these percentages give a reasonably correct impression of the variations in the distribution of sokemen over the wide area comprised within the modern counties of Lincoln, Nottingham, Derby, and Leicester.

The great county of Lincoln fell in 1086, and for administrative purposes still falls, into three divisions, known at the present time as the parts of Lindsey, Kesteven, and Holland. Lindsey, the most northerly of these divisions, fell into three Ridings. The West Riding, which stretched from Lincoln to the Humber, contained six wapentakes. Further east, the North Riding, which also bordered on the Humber, contained five wapentakes, and the South Riding, which lay between the North Riding, the North Sea, and the river Witham, contained eight. The Parts of Kesteven, which contained eleven wapentakes, were bounded on the north by the Fosse Dyke and the Witham, on the east by the Fens, and on the west touched the adjacent parts of Rutland, Leicestershire, and Nottinghamshire. The three wapentakes of Holland formed a rich, but isolated region between the Fens on the west and south and the Wash on the east, connected with the South Riding of Lindsey by a somewhat narrow strip of firm ground, the wapentake of Skirbeck to the north-east of Boston. Any systematic study of the Danelaw must begin with the recognition of the vast differences of topography and soil, and therefore of settlement, which existed in the Middle Ages between the several parts of Lincolnshire.

The remaining counties of this region are far smaller. Leicestershire contained only four wapentakes in 1086. Nottinghamshire falls naturally into two great divisions separated by the river Trent. To the north of the river there were five wapentakes at the date of Domesday Book, to the south there were three. In Derbyshire there were six wapentakes at a later time, but the Domesday survey of this county does not include any exact enumeration of wapentakes, and the number which existed in 1086 remains uncertain. This uncertainty does not materially affect the present study, since, whatever the reason, the number of sokemen recorded in this county is very small.

The tables which follow give the percentage of sokemen to villeins and bordars in each wapentake of the region under consideration.

LINCOLNSHIRE

West Riding

LINDSEY	Aslacoe Wapentake	51·3
	Axholme Wapentake	33·5
	Corringham Wapentake	42·1
	Lawress Wapentake	48·8
	Manley Wapentake	43·8
	Well Wapentake	42·7

North Riding

Bradley Wapentake   68·0

	Haverstoe Wapentake	58·8
	Ludborough Wapentake	73·4
	Walshcroft Wapentake	60·6
	Yarborough Wapentake	48·1

South Riding

	Bolingbroke Wapentake	71·3
	Calcewath Wapentake	44·6
	Candleshoe Wapentake	55·9
	Gartree Wapentake	63·3
	Hill Wapentake	61·7
	Horncastle Wapentake	48·0
	Louth Eske Wapentake	62·5
	Wraggoe Wapentake	47·8
KESTEVEN	Aswardhurn Wapentake	64·6
	Aveland Wapentake	46·6
	Beltisloe Wapentake	33·7
	Boothby Wapentake	55·3
	Flaxwell Wapentake	62·7
	Graffoe Wapentake	48·2
	Langoe Wapentake	45·3
	Loveden Wapentake	46·5
	Ness Wapentake	41·0
	Threo Wapentake	65·1
	Winnibriggs Wapentake	38·1
HOLLAND	Elloe Wapentake	19·9
	Kirton Wapentake	41·9
	Skirbeck Wapentake	46·8

1926

LEICESTERSHIRE

Framland Wapentake	50·0
Gartree Wapentake	30·7
Gosecot Wapentake	27·1
Guthlaxton Wapentake	26·7

NOTTINGHAMSHIRE

NORTH OF TRENT	Bassetlaw Wapentake	25·3
	Broxtow Wapentake	10·7
	Lide Wapentake	33·9
	Oswardbeck Wapentake	45·4
	Thurgarton Wapentake	16·1
SOUTH OF TRENT	Bingham Wapentake	30·5
	Newark Wapentake	52·6
	Rushcliffe Wapentake	32·9

DERBYSHIRE

Appletree Wapentake	Under 1
High Peak Wapentake	0
Morlestone Wapentake	9·2
Repton Wapentake	3·9
Scarsdale Wapentake	11·9
Wirksworth Wapentake	0

In identifying these wapentakes on a modern map, it should be noted that the present wapentake of Sparkenhoe in Leicestershire was created out of the Domesday wapentake of Guthlaxton. The name Sparkenhoe first occurs in a fragment of a survey of Leicestershire of the reign of Henry I (British Museum, Sloane Roll, xxxi. 7), printed by The Department of English Local History among their Occasional Papers, published by the University College, now The University of Leicester, ed. C. F. Slade 1956. In Nottinghamshire, the Oswardbeck wapentake of Domesday is virtually identical with the North Clay division of Bassetlaw wapentake, and Lide wapentake is now represented by the Northern division of Thurgarton wapentake.

In considering these figures it is important to remember that the relative proportion of different social classes is never determined by geographical facts alone. The detailed study of Domesday shows conclusively that sokemen were most numerous upon estates of one particular type, consisting of a central manor with many appurtenant members, often scattered over a wide area. Within these members the rural population was predominantly free, bound to the head manor by suit of court and the render of yearly payments. It is men of this type whom Domesday describes as sokemen, and estates of this type in 1086 and for centuries afterwards were known as sokes. With reference to the preceding tables, the extraordinarily high proportion of sokemen within the wapentake of Bolingbroke is in great part due to the fact that most of this wapentake was included in the soke of Bolingbroke. In Nottinghamshire, the soke of Newark included a large number of the sokemen returned in Domesday under the wapentake of that name. In Leicestershire, the high proportion of sokemen in Framland wapentake is largely due to the great soke of Melton Mowbray. Conversely, several wapentakes would show a considerably higher proportion of sokemen but for the existence of one or two large and centralized manors, in which the bulk of the inhabitants were personally unfree. Although it seems certain that the sokemen of the Danelaw represent, as a class, the rank and file of the Scandinavian armies which had settled this district in the ninth century, two centuries had passed before the social condition of the district was described in Domesday, and there was plenty of opportunity for changes to arise in the relative proportion of different peasant ranks.[1]

One remarkable fact brought out by these tables deserves a separate note. In Derbyshire the proportion of sokemen, never high, becomes negligible in Appletree wapentake in the south-west, and the class ceases to appear in the wapentakes of High Peak and Wirksworth further north. This important difference cannot be due to any change in the methods of enumerating different classes introduced by the local juries of Derbyshire. The proportion of sokemen is actually higher in Scarsdale wapentake in the north-east of Derbyshire than in the adjacent Broxtow wapentake in the west of Nottinghamshire. It is no doubt true that the population of the uplands of north Derbyshire, free and

[1] The sokes of the Danelaw are not merely of interest to the student of medieval history. They played an important part in local government during the seventeenth and eighteenth centuries. The soke of Peterborough in north Northamptonshire, outside the region covered by this study, is still a unit of local administration. I may observe that my father, who was steward of the soke, or 'liberty' of Southwell and Scrooby in Nottinghamshire, held in that capacity courts which represented the rights of jurisdiction possessed over his estates by Osketill, Archbishop of York, in the mid tenth century.

unfree, can never have been high. But even here, free peasants appear in considerable number at a later time, and in Appletree wapentake the general agrarian conditions seem to have been quite favourable to the existence of a free peasant population. The reason for the disappearance of the sokeman in west Derbyshire is probably political rather than agrarian. Derbyshire, like Staffordshire and Cheshire to the west and Yorkshire to the north, was laid waste by William the Conqueror in the winter of 1069. It is safe to assume that here, as in the other counties visited at that time, innumerable free peasants lost their independence as a result of the poverty into which they were thrown by the burning of their farms and the destruction of their stock. In Yorkshire, free landowners of moderate condition and native ancestry appear in large numbers in the course of the twelfth century, and the same is true of Derbyshire. But the Yorkshire Domesday shows that for a long time they were too impoverished to contribute to the taxation which was the main reason for the making of the Domesday survey. It is probable that in Derbyshire also they had not recovered in 1086 from the catastrophe of 1069. This explanation will also account for the fact that it is in the north and west of Derbyshire that the sokemen disappear, for these are the parts of this county nearest Staffordshire and Yorkshire, which felt the full force of the great harrying, and in which therefore recovery would take place most slowly.

But when all reservations have been made, the figures

contained in the tables which have been given remain extremely suggestive. Within a wide and continuous area, half the population recorded by Domesday consisted of sokemen. In Lincolnshire, this area includes the two coast wapentakes of Bradley and Haverstoe on the Humber and stretches westwards through Walshcroft wapentake into Aslacoe wapentake in the West Riding. Southwards, it includes the small wapentake of Ludborough, where the sokemen amount to 73 per cent, and the great wapentake of Louth Eske, where in the twelfth and thirteenth centuries there is better evidence for the existence of a large free peasant population than elsewhere in the whole Danelaw if not in the whole of England.[1] The coast below Louth Eske wapentake is occupied by Calcewath wapentake, where the sokemen fall to 44 per cent. But inland from Louth Eske wapentake and stretching south eastwards to Candleshoe wapentake on the coast again, the wapentakes of Gartree, Hill, and Bolingbroke contain a proportion of sokemen never less than 61 per cent. To the south of this area comes the river Witham and the wide fens along its banks. Beyond this barrier, in Kesteven, lie the adjacent wapentakes of Aswardhurn, Threo, Flaxwell, and Boothby,

[1] The numerous charters relating to this wapentake which are included in the Calendar will illustrate this point. It may be added that hundreds of thirteenth-century grants of small parcels of land by men who were obviously peasants of this district are contained in the series of Ancient Deeds transferred to the Public Record Office from the archives of the Duchy of Lancaster. All that has been attempted here is to calendar the small proportion of these charters in which there is evidence from personal names that the grantor was a man of native origin.

where the proportion of sokemen varies between 55 and 65 per cent. In the four wapentakes of Graffoe, Loveden, Winnibriggs, and Beltisloe, on the western border of Kesteven, the proportion of sokemen is somewhat lower. But in Graffoe wapentake it still amounts to 48 per cent. Graffoe wapentake adjoins the Nottinghamshire wapentake of Newark on the west, where sokemen amount to 52 per cent, and Newark wapentake adjoins the Leicestershire wapentake of Framland, where for once in that county the proportion of sokemen rises to 50. These figures must be significant. They suggest very strongly that the great strength of that Scandinavian settlement from which the free medieval peasantry of the Danelaw is ultimately de-rived lay in central Lincolnshire, that the invaders thinned out to north, south, and west, but that throughout the northern Danelaw the settlement was on a scale sufficient to determine the whole future social development of the re-gion. For the social history of the Danelaw is essentially the history of the Domesday *sochemanni* and their descendants.

In tracing the later course of this history the student finds his chief difficulty in the obscurity of the twelfth century. The surveys of the thirteenth and fourteenth centuries reveal masses of free peasants hardly inferior in number to those recorded in Domesday Book itself. But it is still difficult to connect the eleventh and thirteenth centuries. The Calendar which forms the second part of this study is an attempt to bring together some of the evidence which relates to this obscure intervening period.

Among all the liberties enjoyed by the free peasantry of the Danelaw, the power of alienating their lands was perhaps the most important. A very cursory reading in the cartularies of the religious houses of this region, such as those of Kirkstead, Alvingham, or Bardney, will bring to notice a number of grants of land made by men whose names prove their native, Anglo-Scandinavian, origin, who were obviously peasants, but as obviously free and independent of manorial control. One example of these grants may be introduced here, others will be given later as an appendix to this study:

Notum sit omnibus qui audiunt uel legunt hanc cartam quod ego Henricus filius Toue de Askeby concessi et dedi et hac mea carta confirmaui deo et ecclesie sancte Marie de Kirkesteda et monachis eiusdem loci in puram et perpetuam elemosinam i acram terre arabilis et quartam partem i acre Et iacent in hiis locis scilicet ex west parte uille quicquid habui super Theny iuxta terram Eddrici [*sic*] ex est parte uille ii perticate in latum iuxta terram Eudonis filii Normanni inter duas uias cum pastura ad tantundem terre pertinente Hoc autem warantizabimus ego et heredes mei predictis monachis contra omnes homines inperpetuum. ut habeant et teneant libere et quiete ab omni seculari seruitio et consuetudine et exactione Hiis testibus Willelmo capellano de Askeby Rogero filio Normanni de Askeby Walone de Askeby Henrico filio Eudonis Simone de Kirkesteda. (Cott. Vesp. E xviii, f. 174b.)

Here there is no doubt as to the personal freedom or the tenurial independence of the grantor. He promises to warrant his gift to the monks, he must therefore have other lands which he can give them if his title to the land which is the subject of this charter is successfully challenged. Moreover the ability to warrant a grant of land implied a standing in the courts of wapentake or shire, it implied also the right of appearing before the king's justices when they visited the county.[1] The ability to make a grant in pure and perpetual alms, free and quit from earthly service, custom, and exaction, is no less significant. It shows that the grantor was not subject to any seignorial authority which could insist that he should retain the whole of his tenement in his own hands for his lord's benefit. The grant of pasture rights proves that the grantor was the member of a village community and was able to deal with his fellows in regard to the admission of a new person into the benefit of the commons and wastes of the village. A man who could make a grant in such terms as these was as fully free as anyone could be under the conditions which prevailed in early medieval England.

It is, of course, more difficult to come to any certain conclusion with regard to the history and antecedents of

[1] Little attention has hitherto been given in England to the diplomatic of private charters in the early Middle Ages. The subject is important, not only in itself, but because the study of the development of formulas helps very materially towards dating texts which are only preserved in later copies. The dates which are appended to individual charters in the Calendar which follows are to a great extent founded upon the formulas in which the charters are expressed. The dating of charters by diplomatic methods is particularly important when the charters themselves are made by men of peasant status, whose names do not occur in other sources. A discussion of the formulas of twelfth- and early thirteenth-century charters will be found in the introduction to the volume of *Gilbertine Charters* published by the Lincoln Record Society (vol. 18).

the numerous people who made grants of this nature in the Danelaw. At best, in the majority of cases, it is only possible to establish a reasonable probability. In the present case, the native origin of the grantor is sufficiently proved by his father's name. Tove, well recorded in various forms in both East and West Scandinavian, was not one of the Danish names which the Normans were using at the time of their invasion of England. Its use in Lincolnshire must be due to its survival from the time before the Norman Conquest, and a man who bore it may safely be regarded as a peasant of ancient, local, stock. His ancestors must be represented in Domesday, and the Domesday description of the village of West Ashby, to which the charter relates, is very suggestive. It was divided into three parts, of which the chief was a member of the king's great soke of Horncastle. The village contained in 1086 a population of 45 sokemen, 10 *villani*, and 18 *bordarii*. In view of the obvious freedom of Henry son of Tove, in view also of the fact, brought out by study of the Kirkstead cartulary, that he was only one among many peasants in that place capable of making grants by charter, it can safely be concluded that his ancestors were returned among the 45 sokemen who dwelt there in 1086.

Nevertheless, though free, he should not be regarded as wealthy. The tenements of the medieval sokemen of Lincolnshire were remarkably small, a bovate, twenty acres of arable, was the normal holding of a man of this class. This combination of marked personal and tenurial independence with an economic position inferior to that of an ordinary serf in the south of England is one of the more anomalous features presented by the free peasantry of the Danelaw. It makes all the more remarkable their success in maintaining their position through all the changes of the eleventh and twelfth centuries. Here and there some individual family can be traced increasing its possessions until it passed definitely from the peasant into the knightly class. The family bearing the surname Galle, which appears on many occasions in the following Calendar under Louth Eske Wapentake, took this step in the course of the thirteenth century. But it was very exceptional. In general, the sokeman of the Danelaw, though ready enough to consolidate his position by the sale or exchange of land, seems to have been well content with his peasant condition. He and his fellows were a conservative race. They would resist any encroachment on their ancient liberties. Many features of the agrarian economy of this region in the sixteenth century undoubtedly descend directly from the time before the Norman Conquest. No less significant, though less observed by modern students, is the conservatism with which they preserved the personal names which they inherited from their pre-Conquest ancestors into a time when elsewhere in England the triumph of the French nomenclature introduced in the eleventh century was almost complete.[1] The personal names which occur in the

---

[1] The materials which prove this survival are numerous, varied, and scattered. They include dozens of unpublished cartularies and hundreds of original charters. Up to the present no attempt has been made to publish

Calendar will provide an indication of the volume though hardly perhaps of the variety of this surviving Anglo-Scandinavian nomenclature. The survival is a fortunate circumstance, for it enables a modern inquirer to feel more confident than would otherwise be possible that he is dealing in given cases with men of local origin and ancestry. One inexplicable exception to this conservatism in nomenclature should indeed be noted. In Leicestershire, for reasons which lie almost beyond conjecture, the representatives of the sokemen of 1086, while retaining much of their ancient independence, abandoned the Anglo-Scandinavian names of their ancestors at a very early date. For the rest, in the hills of north Derbyshire as in the Holland Fens, these ancient names occur frequently in the twelfth century, sporadically in the thirteenth, and provide one of the most interesting illustrations which can be given of the continuity of peasant life in this wide region.

The Calendar of charters which will shortly follow represents a collection of documents in which the grantor is proved by his name or by other internal evidence to belong to the native, Anglo-Scandinavian, stock of the Danelaw. It

a collection of this material. The interest of such a collection would be varied. It would demonstrate the strength of Scandinavian influence in the Danelaw, and the sharp distinction which still existed in the twelfth and thirteenth centuries between the Danelaw and the rest of England. It would also reveal differences, perhaps of much historical significance, between the different parts of the Danelaw itself—between Lincolnshire, for example, and Norfolk. It would provide, for the first time, a body of material adequate in volume for the technical study of Anglo-Scandinavian personal nomenclature.

has taken nearly fifteen years to make the collection, and even now it is certainly not exhaustive of the material which might be obtained by further search. It is, however, probable that new discoveries are not likely to destroy the impression produced by the distribution of the documents. It will, in particular, be noticed that a wholly exceptional number of charters is derived from the wapentake of Louth Eske, on the coast of Lincolnshire. It is doubtful whether any similar series could be obtained from any other part of England. The remarkable fact is that every collection of charters relating to this somewhat limited district reveals the same features. The muniments of Lincoln cathedral, the cartularies of Alvingham and Kirkstead, the archives of the Duchy of Lancaster, all have produced grants of small parcels of land made by peasants bearing names which prove their native origin. It is certain that the discovery of fresh material relating to this wapentake would produce additions to the series given here. The cartulary of Louth Park priory, for instance, has disappeared. But a synopsis of the grants which this house received in the twelfth and early thirteenth centuries entered in the Charter Rolls of Edward II shows the free peasant of native descent making grants by charter in very considerable numbers. It would therefore seem that somewhat unusual conditions prevailed within this wapentake. To some extent they can be recovered. Within the wapentake lay the soke of Gayton, one of the largest estates of this kind within the Danelaw. Its lord in the twelfth and early thirteenth centuries was the

Count of Brittany. He was, naturally, non-resident, and it was therefore easy for the men of the soke to maintain their ancient rights and privileges.[1] It is significant that in the wapentake of Skirbeck, where the counts of Brittany possessed another large soke, large numbers of peasants in the thirteenth century still exercised their power of granting land by charter.

But to a great extent the distribution of material is governed by the accidental preservation of texts. Most of the charters abstracted in the Calendar come from the cartularies of religious houses. The records of the Duchy of Lancaster form the one great source of non-monastic provenance which is represented here. Largely, no doubt, by chance, the cartularies of Lincolnshire religious houses have been preserved to a greater extent than those which relate to Nottinghamshire or Derbyshire. The Lincolnshire series is far from complete. There is no record, for instance, of any cartulary of Revesby abbey in the soke of Bolingbroke, which is a main reason why no charters from Bolingbroke wapentake are included in this collection. But a brief glance at the Calendar will show the extent to which the collection is derived from Lincolnshire materials. Two of

[1] It is significant that in the middle of the twelfth century Conan, Duke of Britanny and Earl of Richmond, the lord of Gayton soke, confirmed to the men of the soke all the liberties which they enjoyed in the time of Count Stephen his grandfather, that is, in the time of Henry I (*Ancient Charters*, Pipe Roll Society, vol. 10, p. 54). In 1086, the soke had belonged to the king, in 1066, it had belonged to Edith, wife of King Edward the Confessor. Lordship of this exalted sort was very favourable for the preservation of ancient rights by the peasants subject to it.

the most important Nottinghamshire cartularies, those of Lenton and Worksop, were burned by chance in the eighteenth century before any transcript of them had been made. Most of the monasteries in this county were small, and it is possible that in some of them no cartulary was ever written. Much the same may be said of the lesser monasteries of Derbyshire, though there are other reasons, which have already been indicated, why this county is less fully represented in this collection than might have been expected. In the study of the free peasantry of the Danelaw, as in regard to most matters of early agrarian history, results must inevitably be governed by the irregular distribution of material.

The whole of the preceding paragraphs relate to the great class of sokemen, to a class, that is, whose members may accurately be described as peasants. But other men appear in this collection to whom this term cannot be applied. Swan son of Magnus of Cockerington, whose position is described in a note, must have been a man of considerable wealth. William son of Grimkell of Great Sturton could grant away sixty acres, three bovates of average size, in a single charter. In Derbyshire, men of native origin but of local importance seem from the extant material to have been more numerous than in any other of the shires with which this study is concerned. Walthef of Monsall, Swen son of Ailric of Ballidon, above all, Robert son of Toli of Kniveton, were obviously of more distinguished standing than the peasants whose charters form the bulk of the present collection. The interest of these Derby-shire landowners is of a different sort. If the Lincolnshire peasants represent sokemen of the eleventh century, it may be said that the Derbyshire landowners of the type of Robert son of Toli represent thegns of the same period. It is not hard to find a reason for their appearance in the twelfth century. A man of thegnly rank was much more likely than a sokeman to maintain his social, and something of his economic position in the resettlement of this county after its harrying in 1069. In Yorkshire, genealogical research has proved a definite connection between several twelfth-century landowners of the type under discussion and men who were holding 'manors' in the county on the eve of the Conquest, in 1066.[1] At present, none of the men who appear in this collection can be connected genealogi-cally with landowners of the time before the Conquest. But the evidence suggests very clearly that in the northern parts of the region with which this study deals, individuals of the Old English landowning aristocracy might transmit their social position, and much of their property, to descen-dants who would play a part of their own in the complex society of the twelfth century.

The Calendar which follows attempts to give all the significant information contained in the individual charters relating either to the grantor or to the land which is the subject of the document. The specific references to a clause

[1] Examples may easily be found among the persons who appear as considerable landowners in south Yorkshire in the charters printed by the late Dr. Farrer in *Early Yorkshire Charters*, vol. iii (Lascy Fee).

of warranty, to the fact that the grantor has sealed his charter, to the consent of his heirs, are included because they throw some light on his social position. Notes are inserted from time to time, when the charter raises questions of particular interest or difficulty. Charters of the twelfth and thirteenth centuries are rarely dated. The dates appended to the abstracts in the Calendar must be regarded as only approximate. As has already been observed in a note, they are chiefly based on the nature of the formulas which are contained in the texts, though, of course, attention has been paid to any external information which may throw light on the date of a document. Field names are always given in the form in which they occur in the manuscript, and the name of the village to which a charter refers is also given at least once in the manuscript form whenever this differs in any material respect from the modern spelling. For the sake of clearness, the modern form is used in the abstracts. The references are given in the form which would produce the documents in question at the places where they are preserved.

The appendix of charters which follows the Calendar is derived from two sources, the early thirteenth-century cartulary of Kirkstead abbey and the fourteenth-century cartulary of Thurgarton priory. It seemed more profitable to give the complete series of relevant charters derived from two distinct collections than to make a selection derived from miscellaneous sources. Neither of these cartularies is likely to be printed for a very considerable time. The two series which have been chosen are well contrasted. The Kirkstead charters, as a group, belong to a period which centres on the year 1200. The Thurgarton charters as a whole are later, and therefore illustrate very clearly the long-continued survival of native personal names among the free peasantry of the Danelaw.

The charters which form the subject of the following calendar are derived from the following sources:

British Museum

Cott. Faust. B i. Cartulary of Barlings abbey, Lincolnshire. (14th cent.)

Cott. Nero E vii. Cartulary of Walsingham priory, Norfolk. (14th cent.)

Cott. Tib. C ix. Cartulary of Waltham abbey, Essex. (13th cent.)

Cott. Vesp. E xviii. Cartulary of Kirkstead abbey, Lincolnshire. (13th cent.)

Cott. Vesp. E xx. Cartulary of Bardney abbey, Lincolnshire. (Early 14th cent.)

Lansd. MS. 415. Cartulary of Garendon abbey, Leicestershire. (13th cent.)

Harl. MS. 742. Cartulary of Spalding priory, Lincolnshire. (15th cent.)

Harl. MS. 1063. Cartulary of Rufford abbey, Nottinghamshire. (Early 15th cent.)

Harl. MS. 3640. Cartulary of Welbeck abbey. Nottinghamshire. (14th cent.)

Harl. MS. 3759. Cartulary of Blyth priory, Nottingham-shire. (Late 13th cent.)

Harl. MS. 2110. Cartulary of Castle Acre priory, Nor-folk. (*Circa* 1300.)

Harl. MS. 6118. Extracts (seventeenth century) from cartulary of Bullington priory, Lincolnshire.

Add. MS. 6714. Nineteenth-century transcript of cartulary of Tutbury priory, Staffordshire.

Charters have also been derived from the Cotton, Harleian, and Additional series of charters in the British Museum.

Public Record Office

Ancient Deeds. Cited as AD, with a following letter denoting the series.

Duchy of Lancaster, Cartae Miscellaneae. Charters from the muniments of the Duchy, now bound up in books. Include many charters which would naturally belong to the series lettered L among the Ancient Deeds.

Augmentation office Miscellaneous Books. Original charters bound up in books.

Oxford, Bodleian Library

Laud MS. 642. Cartulary of Alvingham priory, Lincoln-shire. (Late 13th cent.)

MS. Top. Lincoln d 8. Cartulary of Nun Cotham priory, Lincolnshire. (14th cent.)

One charter, No. 210, is derived from the series of charters relating to Stixwould priory, Lincolnshire, recently acquired by this library.

Manchester, Rylands Library

Registrum Eboracense, cited as Reg. Ebor., Cartulary of St. Mary's abbey, York. (14th cent.)

Lincoln, Muniments of Dean and Chapter

Registrum Antiquissimum, cited as Reg. Ant. The oldest (early thirteenth century) cartulary of the cathedral body.

Cartae Decani. Cartulary of the estates appropriated to the Dean. (14th or 15th cent.)

Kniveton Leiger. Cartulary of the Derbyshire family of Kniveton. (14th cent.) [The Lincoln Record Society is printing The Lincoln Charters.]

Original charters. Cited by the reference D. & C. Linc., followed by the press mark of the charter. [Nine volumes of Lincoln Charters are now in print arranged in accordance with the *Registrum Antiquissimum* and under that title. I have noted also under that title where one of these charters appears in the Calendar.]

Southwell Cathedral

Cartulary of Thurgarton priory, Nottinghamshire. (14th cent.)

The published sources from which material has been drawn include:

Jeayes, *Descriptive Catalogue of Derbyshire Charters*, London, 1906.

Stenton, *Danelaw Charters, British Academy*, 1920.

—— *Transcripts of Charters relating to Gilbertine Houses, Lincoln Record Society*, vol. xviii (1922).

Lincolnshire Notes and Queries, vol. xvii.

Dugdale, *Monasticon Anglicanum*, London, 1846.

Madox, *Formulare*, London, 1702.

Facsimiles of Charters in the British Museum, vol. I.

The dates assigned to the unprinted cartularies included in the preceding list are only approximate, and are only intended to give a general indication of the relative age of the different sources of material used for this collection.

The charters in the Calendar are arranged under wapentakes in the alphabetical order of the villages to which they relate. In Lindsey, the wapentakes are arranged alphabetically under the ridings to which they belong, and the alphabetical arrangement of the wapentakes is continued under the Parts of Kesteven and Holland and the counties of Nottingham and Derby. For convenience of reference the abstracts are numbered consecutively, and the arabic numerals prefixed to the charters printed in full in the Appendix relate to the position of each charter in the Calendar.

LINCOLNSHIRE

LINDSEY WEST RIDING

Aslacoe Wapentake

Coates near Ingham

1. Robert f. Gamelli de Cothes

   Grants to Welbeck abbey, in free, pure, and perpetual alms, 4 selions of arable and 5 *perticatae* of meadow in Cotes.

   Warranty.

   Sealing clause.

   Mid thirteenth century   Harl. MS. 3640, f. 101b

2. Robert f. Gamelli de Cothes

   Grants to the same, in free, pure, and perpetual alms, 1 selion in Fillingham.

   Warranty.

   Sealing clause.

   Mid thirteenth century   Ibid., f. 103b

3. Suan . . . et heredes sui

   Are recorded to have granted to Welbeck abbey 5 acres on each side the village of Coates. They will warrant this gift.

   In confirmation by Peter de Chotes, *circa* 1160.

   Ibid., f. 176

Willoughton

4. Roger f. Swein de Wilweton

Quitclaims to the abbey of St Nicholas of Angers a bovate and a half in Willoughton which he claimed against them in the county of Lincoln by the king's writ. Sealing clause.

Mid thirteenth century   Harl. MS. 742, f. 266b

Axholme Wapentake

Owston

5. Thorald f. Ouiet de Oustun

Grants to Sulby abbey the moiety of the toft which he held of Roger de St. Martin in Kinnardferry.

Circa 1200   Danelaw Charters no. 402

Lawress Wapentake

Dunholme

6. Thomas f. Augmundi de Dunham

Grants to William of Nettleham, for his homage and service, 1 acre to the east and another to the west of the village of Dunholme, for a yearly rent of 1 penny. Warranty.

Circa 1180–90   Cott. Vesp. E xviii, f. 202b

7. Brictiue de Dunham

1. Grants to William de Croymar half a bovate of her marriage portion at a yearly rent of a pair of gloves and a pound of cummin.

Consideration: three marks.

Brictiue has sworn before the parish of Dunham to observe this *conventio*.

Early thirteenth century   Cott. Vesp. E xviii, f. 202b

8. Brictiua quondam uxor Tholardi [*sic*] de Duneham

   2. As Brictiua quondam uxor Tholardi [*sic*] de Duneham confirms to Kirkstead abbey the gift which Thorald her husband and afterwards William de Croymare made to that house; namely half a bovate of her marriage portion in Dunholme, in free, pure, and perpetual alms. Sealing clause.

   Circa 1220   Ibid., f. 204b

9. Richard f. Thorald Cok de Dunham

   Grants to Kirkstead abbey a bovate in Dunholme, in free and perpetual alms, at a yearly rent of 4 shillings to the lord of the fee for all service *excepto forensi seruitio octo scilicet denariorum quod uocatur Rasengeld*.

   Sealing clause.

   Circa 1220   Ibid., f. 205

10. Richard f. Thorald Cok de Dunham

    Quitclaims to the same the land of his father in Dunholme which Martin of Dunholme formerly held of Michael Coffin.

    Circa 1220   Ibid., f. 205b

11. Richard f. Thorald Cok de Dunham

    Quitclaims to the same half a bovate in Dunholme which Thorald de Neville gave to Hugh son of Adam,

Richard's *avunculus*, and Nicholas, Hugh's brother, held after him until his death. Richard also quitclaims to the same the acre which Thorald de Neville gave to Hugh son of Adam in augmentation of the aforesaid half bovate. To hold of the chief lord of the fee at a yearly rent of 2 shillings and 6 pence.

Circa 1220   Ibid., f. 205

Nettleham

12. Ivo f. Ulf

Grants and quitclaims to master Malger of Newark, in the court of the Bishop of Lincoln, all the land which he had in Netelham.

Consideration: 15 marks.

Heirs' consent.

Sealing clause. Strip for seal.

1162–6   D. & C. Linc. Dii 84/2/10 [Now printed *Registrum Antiquissimum*, vol. ii no. 613.]

By a charter written in the same hand at the same time Bishop Robert of Lincoln confirms to master Malger of Newark, his clerk, the *mansio* with 4 bovates which Ulf formerly held in Nettleham, for the yearly rent of 10 shillings and 6 pence which Ulf used to render. The Bishop notifies that Ivo son of Ulf has deraigned this tenement against the heirs and wife of Godwin who had unjustly occupied it, and has granted and quitclaimed it in his court to the aforesaid Malger.   (Ibid., 84/2/13. [*R.A.* ii no. 614.])

Scampton

13. Robert f. Agemundi de Scamtun

    Grants to Kirkstead abbey in pure and perpetual alms,
    2 selions in Scampton, and notifies his former gift of
    1 bovate and a half and 1 headland, and 1 selion of
    half an acre in Scampton.

    Warranty of all these gifts.

    Seal Ornate lys + OMNI TEMPORE DILIGIT QUI AMI-
    CUS EST

    Early thirteenth century   Harl. Chart. 55 G 27

NORTH RIDING

Bradley Wapentake

Swallow

14. Henry f. Haconis de Swalue

    Grants to Nun Cotham priory, in pure and perpetual
    alms, until the end of the world, 2 selions in Swallow and
    pasture for 40 sheep.

    Consent of wife and heirs.

    Warranty.

    Late twelfth century   MS. Top. Linc. d 1, f. 11

Haverstoe Wapentake

Wold Newton

15. Hugh f. Petri f. Adestani

    Grants to Alvingham priory, in pure and perpetual
    alms, 2 selions, one on the west of the village *super*

Nettelacres, the other, on the east of the village *super Colewang*.

Warranty.

Circa 1220   Laud MS. 642, f. 151

North Thoresby

16. William f. Walthef de Norchotes

Grants and quitclaims to John de Lasci constable of Chester and his heirs 3 bovates and a toft in Thoresbi which Guy de la Val had granted to William. For this grant the Constable has given 20 pounds to William. Warranty.

Seal: SIGILL WIL . . . IL WALTEF.

1211–32   AD L 3012

By AD L 3074 (Danelaw Charters no. 534) Guy de la Val granted to William son of Walthef, his free man: the toft and 3 bovates in North Thoresby which William's father had held, to hold of him at a yearly rent of 10 shillings.

Yarborough Wapentake

South Ferriby

17. Godewin f. Saxi

Is recorded to have given to the nuns of Stixwould 2 bovates of Roger de Mowbray's fee *tempore Regis Henrici ataui, centum annis elapsis*.

In a copy of the lost Hundred Roll of Yarborough Wapentake, 3 Edward I (Bod. Lib. Dodsworth MS.

lxxxix, p. 83b). The grant must have been made in the reign of Henry II.

Goxhill

18. Robert f. Godrici de Gousel

Grants to Newhouse abbey, in pure and perpetual alms a toft and half an acre on each side of the village of Goxhill, held of Robert by Ivo Scakeloc, *heremita*, at a yearly rent of 2 pence, which Robert reserves to himself.

Warranty.

Circa 1210   Newhouse Cartulary (in possession of Lord Yarborough) no. 316.

East Halton

19. Gunnilda f. Gilberti f. Aumundi de Haltun

Confirms to the same the land in East Halton given by Walter her son.

Seal: SIGILL GVNIL . . .

Circa 1210   Harl. Chart. 51 C 2

SOUTH RIDING
Calcewath Wapentake

Mumby

20. Peter f. Gameli de Cumbreworth

Grants to the lady Beatrice of Mumby, daughter of Ralf of Mumby, all the meadow he had in Sautecroft, at a yearly rent of a pair of white gloves.

Consideration: 100 shillings.

Warranty.

Circa 1220   Cott. Faustina B i, f. 38b

Sutton on sea

21. Margaret filia Roberti f. Ulf de Suttun

Grants to Ralf son of Gilbert of Sutton and his heirs, in pure and perpetual alms, 4 selions in Sutton, and a toft, 7 selions, and 2 half selions in Theddlethorpe. To hold of God and the church of St. Clement of Sutton *iure hereditario* at a yearly rent of 2 pence to God and the said church for buying incense.

Warranty.

Tag only for seal.

Circa 1180–90   D. & C. Linc. 87/3/14

22. Ralf f. Haconis de Maubertorp

Acknowledges that he is bound to pay 13 pence yearly to the nuns of Greenfield *ad pitanciam* within the octave of Whitsun for the land in Sutton which he has of their gift. He also notifies that he and his heirs will assign in alms to the nuns whatever lands or tenements they may hereafter acquire, and hold the same of the nuns at a reasonable rent at the aforesaid term.

Sealing clause.

Two slits for seal tags.

Early thirteenth century   Cott. Chart. xxvii. 65

Swaby

23. Robert f. Haldani

Recorded to have given to Greenfield priory 5½ acres of arable and half a rood of marsh in Swaby.

In remission of suit by Rannulf, Earl of Chester and Lincoln after 1217.   Harl. Chart. 52 A 16

Ulceby by Fordington

24. Ralf f. Alani f. Besi

Grants to Kirkstead abbey 2 acres of arable in Ulceby to hold of him and his heirs in pure and perpetual alms. Warranty.

Early thirteenth century   Cott. Vesp. E xviii, f. 21

Candleshoe Wapentake

Burgh le Marsh

25. Richard f. Sired de Burg

Grants to Bullington priory, in pure and perpetual alms, 13 selions in the territory of Gunby.

Warranty.

Seal: Lys SIG . . . RICARDI FILII SIRED.

Circa 1200   *Danelaw Charters* no. 29

26. Rophar f. Grimchel de Burg

Grants to the same his land called Pusecroft, which Simon Brito confirms.

Early thirteenth century   Add. MS. 6118, p. 419b

   This charter is only known through an abstract derived by Gervase Holles from a cartulary of Bullington that is now lost.

Ingoldmells

27. Alan f. Siwad de Maubertorp

    Grants to the commons of the canons of Lincoln, in alms, 2 acres in Ingoldmells.

    Warranty.

    Sealing clause.

    Early thirteenth century

    Reg. Anti. 114 [Now printed *Registrum Antiquissimum*, vi, no. 1839.   Confirmation ibid., no. 1840.] Confirmed by Robert of Tattershall (ibid.).

Wainfleet

28. Walter f. Asceri

    Grants to Walsingham priory, in free, pure, and perpetual alms, one parcel of land containing 5 perches, according to the perch of 16 feet, in breadth, and in length from the port of Wenflet to the land of Rengot the carpenter.

    Warranty.

    Sealing clause.

    Circa 1225   Cott. Nero E vii, f. 129

29. as Walter f. Asceri de Northwenflet

    Grants to Walter f. Ernisii de Suthwenflet one parcel of land of the same size as that described in the previous charter and lying between.

    Warranty.

    Sealing clause.

    Circa 1225   Ibid., f. 129b

Winthorpe

30. Walter f. Haldani de Wegland

Grants to the commons of the church of Lincoln, in pure and perpetual alms, the toft in Winthorpe in which he dwelt.

Warranty.

Tag for seal.

Circa 1200   D. & C. Linc. D ii 88/3/22 [Now printed *Registrum Antiquissimum*, vi, no. 1829.]

31. Ralf f. Magni de Burg

Grants to Bullington priory, in pure and perpetual alms, 30 acres in Winetorp which he deraigned against Aumeric de Pereres in the court of Alan of Martin by the king's writ. The priory shall render yearly 5 shillings to Alan and 2 shillings to Ralf until he either dies or enters religion.

Seal: Bird + SIGILLUM . . . DE BURG.

Circa 1180–90   *Danelaw Charters* no. 112

There exists a mutilated charter by which Hugh le moine of Burgh and Basilla his wife quitclaim the tenement of Magnus to Bullington priory. The legend upon the seal reads + SIGILL' BASIL . . . IE MAGNI (Cott. Chart. xxvii, 121). It would therefore seem that Basilla was Magnus's daughter. The family must have been of more than peasant rank.

Gartree Wapentake

Kirkstead

32. Tori carpentarius Humphrey the clerk Walter Lumbardus; Robert de Apulia; Walter f. Godrici; Gilbert Skerewind

    Release to Kirkstead abbey whatever right they had in certain land between the abbey and Stixwould. They have taken an oath in no way to disturb the monks in respect of this land.

    Circa 1160   Cott. Vesp. E xviii, f. 3b

33. William f. Ketelli William f. Alani nepos eius

    Release to the same all their right in the same land.

    Circa 1160   Ibid.

Hill Wapentake

Hagworthingham

34. Raingot f. Imeri de Hagwrdingham

    Is recorded by Gilbert de Gant, his lord, to have given in alms to the monks of Bardney the church of Hagworthingham which was within the fee of 6 bovates given to the monks by Gilbert's father at the time of his death. Raingot held these 6 bovates of St. Oswald by the sixth of a knight's service, but gave the third part of his land to the monks so that he should from thenceforward hold the remaining two parts of the monks free from all service. It was because he had done them no service for this fee, and could thereafter do them none, that he gave them the aforesaid third part of his land. Gilbert de Gant has confirmed these gifts by this his charter.

Circa 1150   Cott. Vesp. E xx, f. 66

Langton by Partney

35. Reigot f. Wilgirb de Drextorp

Grants to Kirkstead abbey, in pure and perpetual alms, half an acre in the fields of Dexthorpe with another selion in the fields of Langton.

Warranty.

Early thirteenth century

Cott. Vesp. E xviii, f. 21b

36. Eilric de Sazstorp

Grants to the same 2 selions, reckoned as 1 acre, in the fields of Langton.

Warranty.

Early thirteenth century   Ibid., f. 19

Horncastle Wapentake

West Ashby

37. Haldan f. Wluieti de Askeby

Grants to Kirkstead abbey, in free, pure, and perpetual alms, a perch of meadow in Ashby.

Warranty.

Circa 1220   Ibid., f. 175

38. Hugh f. Brunneys de Askeby

Grants to the same, in pure and perpetual alms, one selion, being 2 roods in breadth, in Ashby, with common pasture appurtenant to so much land.
Warranty.
Early thirteenth century   Ibid., f. 172b

39. Henry f. Toue de Askeby

Grants to the same, in pure and perpetual alms, an acre and a quarter of arable in Ashby with pasture appurtenant to so much land.
Warranty.
Early thirteenth century   Ibid., f. 174b

Coningsby

40. Robert f. Swaue de Cuningesbi

Grants to the same, in free, pure, and perpetual alms, half an acre of meadow in the meadows of Coningsby.
Warranty.
Sealing clause.
Early thirteenth century   Harl. Chart. 44 B 17

41. Henry the reeve f. Willelmi f. Yaderici de Cuningbi

Grants to the same, in free, pure, and perpetual alms, his whole toft with houses in Coningsby. To hold of

John son of Ketelbern of Keal at a yearly rent of 16 pence.

Warranty.

Sealing clause.

Circa 1230   Cott. Vesp. E xviii, f. 154

42. Robert f. Thori de Cuninghesbi

Confirms to Kirkstead abbey, in pure and perpetual alms, the gift of Henry son of Walter of Coningsby, namely the moiety of a *cultura*, meadow, and common pasture.

Warranty.

Early thirteenth century   Ibid., f. 148b

43. Roger f. Goddrici

Grants to the same, in alms and fee-farm, a croft in Coningsby, to hold at an annual rent of 4 pence.

Consent of Matelina, Roger's wife.

Warranty.

Affidatio in the hand of Robert, the abbot's man.

Circa 1200   *Danelaw Charters* no. 201

44. William gener Ulf de Cunighesbi

Confirms to the same, in fee-farm and perpetual alms, a fishery in Witham called Aldehida, which the monks formerly held of Ulf, his father-in-law, by his gift. They hold at a yearly rent of 12 pence or 6 sticks of eels. Consent of Maud, William's wife, and his heirs. Warranty.

Affidatio in the hand of Nicholas Bec.

Late twelfth century   Cott. Vesp. E xviii, f. 4

45. Richard f. Sigwardi de Cunighesbi

Grants to the same his portion, namely the fourth part, of the same fishery. To hold in perpetual alms at a yearly rent of 3 halfpence.

Warranty.

Late twelfth century   Ibid., f. 5

Haltham on Bain (Holthaim)

46. Robert f. Suarthoued' et Richilda his wife; Rainald and Ivetta his wife; William and Agnes his wife; and Gunnild sister of these women

Grant to the same that they make their dam, etc., of their mill upon the Bain, touching which works there had formerly been a dispute between them. They have made this grant, in alms, at the time when they were received into the fraternity of that house, and have received from the monks 1 mark for their unanimous gift. They have severally pledged their faith to observe this grant in the hand of Walter the chaplain of Bardney, by the aforesaid mill.

1163   Harl. Chart. 44 E 55

Kirkby on Bain

47. Adelsi de Kyrkeby

Releases to the same all the claim which he had against the monks touching their closes by the mill of Bain, so that they may hold those closes of him and his heirs in perpetual alms.

Early thirteenth century   Cott. Vesp. E xviii, f. 149

48. Roger f. Eylsi de Kyrkeby

Grants to the same an acre of meadow in Kirkby to hold of him and his heirs in perpetual alms.

Warranty.

Circa 1220   Ibid., f. 152

Martin by Horncastle

49. Acke f. Grimkel

Confirms to the same, in pure and perpetual alms, as regards himself and his heirs, a meadow called Dunesholm given them by Geoffrey son of Alberic of Martin with his consent. He will warrant and acquit this meadow against all men, and has pledged his faith to this in the hand of Ketall le Matzun.

Circa 1160   Ibid., f. 145b

This confirmation by Acke is inserted in the first person as a clause in the charter of Geoffrey son of Alberic. Confirmations expressed in this form are rare. Acke is stated by Geoffrey to have been his tenant for the meadow which was the subject of the grant. A tenant's consent to an alienation of his holding by his lord seems to have been required in the twelfth century, but there was no rule defining the formulas in which it should be recorded.

Roughton

50. Robert Calf

(1) Grants to the same, in pure and perpetual alms, a bovate in Roughton which Reginald the white held of the fee of Adelsi f. Bern. To hold at a yearly rent of 3 shillings. He also grants 8 acres of arable in Edlington to hold at a yearly rent of a pound of cummin to John of Edlington for 4 of these acres.

Warranty.

Affidatio in the hand of Warin the chaplain of Tattersall. Tag only for seal.

Circa 1160   *Danelaw Charters* no. 187

51. Robert Calf

(2) Grants to the same, in perpetual alms, half the land which Adelsi f. Bern held of Robert Marmiun's fee in Roughton, being 6 bovates. The whole of Adelsi's demesne is in this moiety. The monks shall acquit this land of danegeld, murder fine, the four aids of the sheriff, and any common geld laid by the king upon the whole county.

Consent of Thomas, Robert's son and heir.

Warranty.

Affidatio as above.

Seal: a calf + SIGILLUM . ROBERTI . WE : EL : :

Circa 1160   *Danelaw Charters* no. 188

52. Robert Calf

(3) Regrants, with additions, the bovate granted by the first charter and the 6 bovates granted by the second.

Consent of Nicholas, Alan, and Herbert, Robert's nephews and heirs, who have pledged their faith with him in the hand of Warin the chaplain of Tattersall.

Warranty.

Seal as appended to preceding charter.

Circa 1175   *Danelaw Charters* nos. 189–90

Upon Robert and the other members of the family to which he belonged see *Danelaw Charters*, Introduction c. By a charter of 1163 Robert Marmiun grants to Kirkstead abbey half the land which Adelsi son of Bern and his *nepos* Asketin f. Od held of him in Roughton (*Danelaw Charters* 186). He states that he has made this gift with the consent of Adelsi's *nepos* Robert Calf, Asketin, Robert's brother, and Ingerid, the mother of Robert and Asketin. This does not establish the full parentage of Robert Calf, but it reveals him in an Anglo-Scandinavian environment.

53. Walter f. Godrici de Ructona

(1) Grants to the same, in pure and perpetual alms, 4 selions in Roughton.
Warranty.
Affidatio in the hand of Robert Calf.
Slit only for seal tag.
Circa 1160   *Danelaw Charters* no. 192

54. Walter f. Godrici de Ructona

(2) Regrants the 4 selions which were the subject of the preceding charter, and also releases his claim in certain land between Kirkstead abbey and Stixwould.
Warranty.
Affidatio in the hand of Robert Calf.
The final witness is Robert, lay brother of Kirkstead, Walter's brother, with whom the latter states that he has made this gift.
Fragment of seal.
Circa 1160   *Danelaw Charters* no. 193

An earlier document entered in the Kirkstead Cartulary recites that Godric f. Gympe gave to the monks 3 acres of arable and half an acre of meadow in Roughton at the time when they received Gympe his father to keep him until his death. The context shows that this Godric was the father of the Walter who made the two charters abstracted above (Cott. Vesp. E xviii, f. 140b).

47

Great Sturton

55. William f. Grimchelli

Grants to the same, in perpetual alms, 60 acres of his inheritance in Sturton, common pasture, and meadow. He will enlarge for the monks a way named Eilouagate in Sturton. He also confirms the gifts of Simon and Robert f. Aki, his kinsmen, and of Hugh the clerk.

1140–7   Cott. Vesp. E xviii, f. 159

William's gift is confirmed by R. de Curci and A. his wife, who assert that it was made in their presence (ibid.).

Louth Eske Wapentake

Alvingham

56. Thorald filius et heres Dued de Aluingham et Gilebertus frater eius

At the request of Gamel their brother grant to Alvingham priory a toft and 13 selions in Alvingham, in pure and perpetual alms, with their brother Gamel, who has taken the habit of religion in the priory.

Warranty.   Laud MS. 642, f. 13

57. Thorald filius et heres Dued de Aluingham et Gilebertus frater eius

Demise to the same the great *daila* of Dued in Tunstalcroft in perpetual fee-farm at a yearly rent of 16 pence.

Warranty.

Circa 1190   Ibid., f. 13

58. As Thorald f. Deued de Aluingham

Grants to the same the toft of Dued his father, with 2 acres of meadow, 16 selions and a headland, to hold of the lord of the fee at a yearly rent of 13 pence and the third of a penny.
Warranty.
Circa 1200   Ibid., f. 13

59. As Thorald f. Duede

Grants to the same a selion called Duederig on the south of Kunigesgate with the meadow belonging to it and 2 other perches of meadow.
Warranty.
Circa 1200   Ibid., f. 13

60. Sunniua quondam uxor Thoraldi f. Duede

Confirms to the same all the lands and meadows which the priory has by the gift of Thorald her late husband.
Sealing clause.
Early thirteenth century   Ibid., f. 13

61. William f. Johannis f. Duede de Aluingham

Grants to the same 1 selion in Alvingham.
Warranty.
Sealing clause.
Circa 1230   Ibid., f. 21b

62. John f. Johannis f. Duede

Quitclaims to the same all the land given by his father, namely 3 selions and a small parcel of meadow.
Warranty.

Circa 1230   Laud MS., 642 f. 21b

63. Robert and William filii Radulfi f. Dued de Aluingham

Grant to the same their whole inheritance in Alvingham, namely the toft of Ralf their father, 2 acres of meadow, 16 selions and a headland, to hold of the lord of the fee at a yearly rent of 13 pence and the third of a penny. The priory has undertaken to receive William into their body when he shall wish.
Consent of heirs.

Circa 1220   Ibid., f. 13

It is evident from these charters that the three sons of 'Dued', Thorald, John, and Ralf, had each received an equal share of a tenement in Alvingham, and that the curious rent of 13 pence and the third of a penny, which is mentioned twice above, represents the third part of a total rent of 40 pence, that is, a quarter of a mark of silver.

64. Ralf f. Thoraldi de Aluingham

Grants to Alvingham priory his whole patrimony in Alvingham, namely a toft and 14 acres of arable, to hold of the lord of the fee at a yearly rent of 18 pence

secundum libertates et consuetudines sokemannorum de Gay-tona . . . quando ceteri sokemani suam firman reddunt.
Warranty.
Early thirteenth century   Ibid., f. 13b

> Gaytona is Gayton le Wold in this wapentake, the head of the soke of which Alvingham was a member.

South Cadeby

65. Eustace de Cathebi and his heirs

> Grant to Kirkstead abbey, in pure and perpetual alms, all the land which Jaalf of Southorpe held of Swan of Cadeby south of the way which goes to Louth. Eustace and his brothers and their heirs have also quitclaimed to the monks the land of William Trig of Saxedale, and will support the monks at their charges against all men who shall lay claim to this land. They have pledged their faith to observe this grant in the hand of Walter the sheriff.

1157–63   Cott. Vesp. E xviii, f. 86

> That Swan of Cadeby was the father of Eustace is proved by a charter of Alan de Baiocis (ibid.) confirming to Kirkstead abbey a *cultura* in Cadeby given by Eustace *filius Swani de Catebi*, his man Between 1190 and 1193 Robert son of Eustace sold to the lady Basilia of Welton a bovate and a half in Welton le Wold, 3 tofts which were Jalf's and the whole of the latter's issue (*Danelaw Charters* no.

168). The Jalf of this charter can safely be identified with the Jaalf of the cartulary text abstracted above. Presumably he was unfree, but he certainly held more property than was usual for a man of his class. Swan of Cadeby was evidently a man of some local importance, though nothing is known of his antecedents.

It may be added that the site of Saxedale is unknown and that South Cadeby is now depopulated. Its position is marked by the foundations of a line of toftsteads still visible in a grass field.

Cockerington

66. Roger Vavasur f. Siwardi de Cokerintona

Grants to William de Redburna and his heirs the toft which William Sanggestere held and half a bovate which Roger held of the fee of William de Fristona, to hold of Roger and his heirs at a yearly rent of 6 pence. Heirs' consent.

Warranty.

Circa 1190   Laud MS. 642, f. 62b

67. Robert f. Sigwardi de Cokerintona

Grants to Alvingham priory, in pure and perpetual alms, the toft which he held of the priory and 5 selions in Cockerington. He also grants to the same half a toft and croft which were formerly his brother's and two-thirds of the land which his brother Roger had held. He has proved his right to the latter land before

the king's justices at Lincoln. The nuns of Alvingham
have received Goda his daughter *ad consiliandam.*
Warranty.
Circa 1190   Ibid., f. 62b

68. As Robert f. Sigwardi de Cokerintun frater Rogeri le
Vavasur et heres

Confirms to Alvingham priory in pure and perpetual
alms the meadows and lands in Cockerington given to
the priory by Roger his brother. He also grants to the
priory the 2 bovates which Hanke and Gille held, and
whatever the nuns have of his inheritance in Cockerington.
Heirs' consent.
Warranty.
Circa 1190   Ibid., f. 63

69. Hachet f. Thoraldi de Chorintun

Confirms to the same all the land which the nuns have
by the gift of his father.
Warranty.
Circa 1200   Ibid., f. 63

70. Hugh f. Anke de Cokerintona

Grants to the same in pure and perpetual alms the
toft which 'Ankus' his father held of the priory.
Warranty.
Sealing clause.
Early thirteenth century   Ibid., f. 61b

71. Yvo f. Suen and his heirs

Confirm to the nuns of Alvingham 7 acres of meadow of Yvo's demesne in Medelcroft, which Suen de Corintun his father before his death gave to the church of Cockerington in satisfaction for a debt. He also confirms to the nuns 7 acres of arable which Suen his father had given them.

Circa 1160   Laud MS. 642, f. 80b

72. As Yuo de Marisco

Grants to the same 4 selions of arable which belong to his fee in Dunnesdale, 2 perches of meadow *iuxta Scothox per medium Hocdeiles*, and a parcel of meadow 20 feet in breadth in Hutcroft. He also confirms whatever arable or meadow Swan *filius Magni* his father, or his own men, have given to the priory. He has pledged his faith to warrant this grant to the priory in perpetual alms.

Circa 1160   Ibid., f. 80b

The position of Ivo de Marisco is of exceptional interest. His father Swan son of Magnus was certainly a man of Anglo-Scandinavian origin. He is called Swan Magnussuna in a confirmation of his gifts to Louth Park Priory (*Calendar of Charter Rolls 8 Edward II*) where the form of his name has a definitely Scandinavian character. On the other hand, Ivo appears as a tenant by military service in the great Return of knight's fees made in 1166 by order of King Henry II (*Red Book of the Exchequer*, p. 388) where it is stated that he held half a knight's fee of Hugh de Bayeux. He died before 1179 leaving a daughter named Christiana who was given in marriage by Hugh de Bayeux, as feudal lord, to Roger de Neville. The charter by which this gift was made was preserved in the Alvingham Cartulary (Laud MS. 642, f. 68). Few twelfth-century documents of this kind have survived, and the present example may be given here at full length: Hugo de Baiocis omnibus hominibus suis Francis et Anglicis tam futuris quam presentibus salutem. Sciatis quod ego reddidi et concessi Rogero de Neuill' totam terram que fuit Yvonis de Marisco in Cokerint' cum omnibus pertinenciis cum filia sua Christiana sicuti idem Yvo eam liberius et quietius tenuit anno et die quo fuit vivus et mortuus, ei et heredibus suis qui de Christiana nascentur. Tenendam de me et heredibus meis in feudo et hereditate faciendo seruicium dimidii militis mihi et heredibus meis. In the whole Danelaw it would be hard to find another family whose history so definitely connects the Anglo-Scandinavian society of the eleventh century with the organized feudalism of the later Middle Ages.

Grainthorpe

73. Richard de Germuntorp f. Baldrici

   (1) Grants to the chapter of Lincoln cathedral, in pure

and perpetual alms, a yearly rent of 6 pence paid him by Rumfar of Grainthorpe son of Robert the palmer and Ralf of Grainthorpe son of Siward for the land which Baldric, Richard's father had within the toft of Arnegrim his uncle, and the land which Baldric had in the toft on the west of Arnegrim's toft, and the land which Baldric had in Caluecroft, and Arnegrim's salt-pan.

Warranty.

Late twelfth century · · · · · · · · · · · · · · · Reg. Ant., f. 89

74. As Richard de Germuntorp f. Basldrici

(2) Grants to the commons of the canons of Lincoln, in pure and perpetual alms, 9 acres lying in 5 places in Grainthorpe.

Warranty.

Sealing clause.

Early thirteenth century · · · · · · · · · · · · · · · Ibid., f. 89b

75. John de Germ'torp f. Hauke

Confirms to the chapter of Lincoln cathedral the gift made with his counsel and assent by Hugh de Holdernesse and Lewara his wife, namely $3\frac{1}{2}$ acres and half a perch in Suthcroft and half an acre of meadow in Cudailles, in pure and perpetual alms.

Warranty.

Late twelfth century · · · · · · · · · · · · · · · Ibid., f. 88

The charter of Hugh of Holdernesse is entered on the following folio. By it Hugh states that he has made his gift *consilio et assensu Leware uxoris mee et sororis Alani f Seldwar'*. The gift is also confirmed by John f. Gikell' de Jerburc, who is known from other sources as a tenant on the fee of the count of Brittany in Lincolnshire. The land in question therefore lay in the part of Grainthorpe which formed a member of Gayton soke, on which in 1086 there had been a population of 13 sokemen and 6 villeins.

76. Ralf f. Liolf de Germethorp

Grants to Alvingham priory, in pure and perpetual alms, the land which he had within defined boundaries in Grainthorpe.

Warranty.

Circa 1250 Laud MS. 642, f. 106b

77. Robert Hopescort and Bart his brother

Grant to the same, in perpetual alms, all the land in Germethorp and Great Grimsby which their brother Tobias had held, with their niece Scicilia [*sic*], daughter of Tobias, whom the nuns of Alvingham have received into their company. Robert and Bart have pledged their faith to warrant this gift in the hand of William f Amfridi de Lekeburne, reserving the services due to the king and the count (of Brittany).

Circa 1190 Ibid., f. 99b

There is no mark of abbreviation after the name Bart in the cartulary, and it may therefore be taken as a form of O.N. Bárðr, O. Dan. Bardh.

78. Seward de Ludeburc et Maria sponsa Sewardi et heres Roberti Hoppescort

    Confirm to the same in perpetual alms 4 acres of meadow in Waterlous daile formerly given by Robert Hoppescort, to hold at a yearly rent of 2 pence. They have pledged their faith in the hand of Ralf the squire of Lambert de Scoteneia to warrant this confirmation to the nuns.

    Assent of Andrew their heir.

    Circa 1200   Laud MS. 642, f. 103

79. Thorald f. Sewardi de Germethorp

    Grants to the same 2 selions of land at a yearly rent of 8 pence.

    Warranty.

    Sealing clause.

    Circa 1240   Ibid., f. 103

80. Alan f. Willelmi f. Rumphari de Germetorp et Galfridus frater eius

    Grant to the same, in free, pure, and perpetual alms, all their land in the place called Stang'mal' in Grainthorpe.

    Warranty.

    Sealing clause.

    Circa 1260   Ibid., f. 108b

Grimoldby

81. Robert f. Edrici Bugge de Grimolby

Grants to the commons of the canons of Lincoln cathedral 2 selions in Grimoldby.

Warranty.

Early thirteenth century   Reg. Ant., f. 86b

Keddington

82. Tocha prepositus de Kedingtun

Grants to Alvingham priory, in pure and perpetual alms, 7 selions of his land in Keddington. He also confirms to the same priory and to its church of St. Margaret of Keddington all the land which was given to that church from his fee.

Warranty.

Consent of Gilbert his son and heir and of his other sons.

Circa 1190   Laud MS. 642, f. 126

83. As Toka de Kedigtun

Grants to the same, in pure and perpetual alms, 4 selions in return for an immediate payment of 11 shillings.

Consent of Geoffrey of Keddington, Toka's lord, and of his heirs. Toka, Geoffrey his lord, and Toka's sons and heirs, namely Brice and his brothers, have made this gift and confirmed it with Geoffrey's seal and pledged their faith to warrant it.

Circa 1190 Laud MS. 642 f. 126

84. Roger f. Mild de Kedigtun

Grants to the same, in pure and perpetual alms, a selion of arable on Buregauilfurlangis.

Warranty.

Sealing clause.

Circa 1230 Ibid., f. 126b

85. As Roger f. Mild'

Grants to the same, likewise in alms, 3 selions in Keddington, in exchange for 1 selion given him by the priory.

Warranty.

Sealing clause.

Circa 1230 Ibid., f. 126b

86. Walter f. Rogeri f. Milde

Grants to the same, in pure and perpetual alms, 4 selions in Keddington.

Warranty.

Circa 1250 Ibid., f. 127

Louth

87. Walter f. Sivat de Luda

Grants to the nuns of Alvingham, in pure and perpetual alms, so much of his land on the north of Louth as may be sufficient to make a road for 2 carts going to and coming from the nuns' quarry.

Heirs' consent.

Warranty.

Late twelfth century   Ibid., f. 132

88. Thomas f. Sywat de Luda

Makes a grant similar to the above, with the consent of Thomas his heir.

Late twelfth century   Ibid., f. 132

Manby

89. Rannulf f. Toraldi de Manneby

Grants to Alvingham priory, in pure and perpetual alms, the toft which Thorald his father held in the village of Manby of the socage (*de socchagio*) of Gayton.

Warranty.

Sealing clause.

Early thirteenth century   Ibid., f. 86b

90. Sibilla and Juliana filie Walteri f. Gunne de Manneby

Grant to the same, in pure and perpetual alms, the whole toft in Manby which Walter their father held of the socage of Gayton.

Warranty.

Sealing clause.

Circa 1225   Ibid., f. 86b

91. Robert f. Quenlof de Manneby

Sells and quitclaims to Andrew son of Odo Galle all his land in Manby, namely a toft, 3 perches of meadow, and 13 selions lying in eight places, to hold *jure hereditario* of Robert and his heirs at a yearly rent of 6½ pence and the third of a halfpenny at the four terms of the year customary in the soke (of Gayton).

Warranty.

Circa 1225   D. of L. Cart. Misc. II 5/4.

92. Gilbert f. Queneluue

Sells to Andrew Galle all his land in Manby, for an immediate payment of 10 marks of silver, to hold of Gilbert and his heirs at a yearly rent of 1 halfpenny rendering also to the Count of Brittany 20 pence yearly for the service due from the aforesaid land.

Warranty.

Sealing clause.

Circa 1230   AD L 2937

The Queneluue of this charter is identical with the Quenlof of the previous one.

Saltfleetby

93. Ketell Dumping

Grants to St. Mary of Lincoln, in pure and perpetual alms, 5 acres of his free land, and with Odo his son offers them upon St Mary's altar. The aforesaid Odo

shall hold these acres hereditarily of God and St. Mary
at a yearly rent of 12 pence.

Sealing clause.

Dated at Whitsuntide 1176

D. & C. Lincoln D ii. 86/2/25[1]

94. Hugh and Oggrim filii Aluerun

Grant to St. Mary of Lincoln, in pure and perpetual
alms, 2 acres of their free land in Rastoluecroft, *in
angulo de suwest*, and offer them upon St. Mary's altar.

Sealing clause.

Dated at Whitsuntide 1176   Reg. Ant., f. 94b

95. Aschel Mudding

Grants to Odo Galle and his heirs 4 acres and half a
perch of meadow upon his 'deila' called Suorthekere,
to hold of Odo and his heirs at a yearly rent of 8 pence.

Consent of heirs.

Warranty.

Late twelfth century   AD L 2792

96. Gunnilda filia Acke Mudding de Salfletby

Releases to Andrew f. Odonis Galle all her right in her

[1] Printed in full in 'The Danes in England', *Collected Papers* pp. 150 f.
Also in the *Registrum Antiquissimum*, vol. v, no. 1630, ed. Kathleen Major.
Lincoln Record Society, vol. 34, 1940.

father's land. For this release Andrew has given her 1 mark of silver in her great necessity.

Seal: SIGILL GVNNILD F AC.

Early thirteenth century   AD L 3052

As the Acke Mudding of this charter is certainly identical with the Aschel Mudding of the previous document it follows that Acke was a recognized short form of Askell in the Northern Danelaw.

97. Robert f. Ascheli

Grants to Philip f. Odonis Galle a parcel of land within defined boundaries, at a yearly rent of a clove gilly-flower.

Warranty.

Circa 1230   AD L 2562

98. Robert f. Willelmi f. Askel de Saltfletby

Grants to the same 1 acre and 24 *fallae* of land in the place called Fiskmare in exchange for 1 acre at the south end of the selion called Milnrich'.

Warranty.

Sealing clause.

Circa 1250   AD L 2749

The Askel of the two last documents is certainly a different person from Askel Mudding above.

99. Robert, Thomas, and Thomas, filii Hugonis f. Goderici de Saulfleteby

Grant to Robert Wisman and his heirs 1 selion lying

in Thirnholm to hold of the grantors and their heirs at
a yearly rent of 2 pence.

Warranty.

Sealing clause.

Three seals are still appended to the document.

Circa 1250   AD L 2886

100. Agnes f. Hugonis f. Goderici de Saltfletby

Releases to Phillip Galle and his heirs all her right by
reason of inheritance or dower in half an acre of land
lying in Thirnolleme.

Warranty.

Sealing clause.

Circa 1260   AD L 2885

The half-acre mentioned here is certainly identical
with the selion of the previous document.

101. Hawisia f. Ragenil de Saltfletby

Confirms to Andrew Galle 3 perches of meadow.
For this confirmation Andrew has given 10 shillings
to Hawisia in her necessity.

Warranty.

Seal.

Circa 1230   AD L 2821

102. Wigot de Holmo

Grants to Siwat f. Hugonis de Halingtun, in free
marriage with Edeyt his daughter, an acre and a half

of meadow at the north end of his strip (*ad nhort partem dayle mee*), to hold of him and his heirs by hereditary right at a yearly rent of 2 pence.

Warranty.

Large round seal with raised margin, legend almost obliterated.

Circa 1210   AD L 2527

103. Siwat de Halingetun

Grants to Hodo Galle and his heirs an acre of meadow which he received in free marriage with his wife to hold of him and his heirs at a yearly rent of 1 penny.

Warranty.

Seal: SIGILL SIWATI FILII HVGON.

Circa 1220   AD L 2832

104. As Sywad de Halinctun

Sells to Andrew f. Odonis Galle and his heirs, for 20 shillings, an acre and a half of meadow, to hold of Sywad and his heirs at a yearly rent of 2 pence.

Warranty.

Seal: SIGILL' SIVADI FIL HVGONIS.

Circa 1230   AD L 2528

These three charters all relate to the same property.

105. Wigot de Holm

Grants to Odo Galle and his heirs six acres of meadow in Neucroft *et unum gaire rosere quod iacet inter A et Adic*, to hold of Wigot and his heirs at a yearly rent of 6 pence.

Consent of wife and heirs.

Warranty.

Seal: SIGILL WIGOTI DE HOLM.

Circa 1200   AD L 2882

106. Walter f. Wygoti de Holm

(1) Confirms to the same the same tenement together with an acre and a half of arable *iacentem super Holm super Hungrehil*, to hold of Walter and his heirs at a yearly rent of 7 pence. In consideration of an immediate payment of a mark of silver Walter has released to Odo 6 pence out of his yearly rent of 7 pence.

Warranty.

Seal: SIGILL WALTERI F WIED.

Circa 1220   AD L 2883

107. Walter f. Wygoti de Holm

(2) Grants to Andrew Galle and his heirs a selion of arable and a rent of 4 pence due to Walter from John *pictor* at the four terms customary in the soke (of Gayton). For this grant, Andrew has given 20 shillings to Walter in his necessity.

Warranty.
Seal.
Circa 1220   AD L 2529

108. Adelilda f. Hialsi de Holmo

Quitclaims by final concord before the king's justices at Lincoln to Walter Galle and his heirs 40 acres in Saltfleetby. For this quitclaim she has received 1 mark.

9 October 1187   AD L 2904

109. Avina f. Adelstan

Grants to the commons of the canons of Lincoln, in pure and perpetual alms, all the land which was her father's to the east of the church of All Saints in Saltfleetby.

General heirs' consent.

Warranty.

Sealing clause.

Oval seal: Lys.

Circa 1200   D. & C. Linc. D ii. 86/2/26 [Now printed *Registrum Antiquissimum*, vol. v, no. 1637]

110. Richard f. Auin and Hugh his brother

Sell to Andrew and his assignees 2 acres of arable with free entry and exit through the middle of their

toft and croft to the royal way, to hold of them and their heirs. Andrew has given them 20 shillings.
Warranty.
One Seal: s' RIC' . FIL' . AVIN EDES and slits for two more tags.
Early thirteenth century   AD L 3154

111. Hungwin f. Aldith
Grants to Reginald his son $3\frac{1}{2}$ acres in Saltfleetby, namely those which Hungwin bought from Robert of Raithby. To hold of Robert as Hungwin's heir at a yearly rent of 10 pence.
Circa 1200   AD L 2677

112. Mathildis f. Yungewyn de Salfletby
Quitclaims to Philip son of Odo Galle all her right and claim in 1 toft and 1 croft and in all the land which was Yungwin, her father's, for 20 shillings.
Sealing clause.
Seal: Ornate lys SIGILL' MA The seal is broken in half. The tag is made of a strip from a charter.
Circa 1220   AD L 2627

113. Alan f. Alicie f. Hyunguini de Salfletebi
Quitclaims to Philip son of Odo Galle all his right and claim in 1 toft and 1 croft which were Reginald, his uncle's for 20 shillings.
Sealing clause.
Seal: Eight-petalled flower. s' ALANI FIL' . . . VN.
Circa 1220   AD L 2626

114. Rannulf f. Getelli

> Grants to Andrew son of Odo Galle of Saltfleetby all his land between that of John son of Odo Dumping on the west and Osbert, the parson's son, and the grave yard of the church of All Saints of Saltfleetby on the east. To hold of him and his heirs at a yearly rent of 4 pence.
>
> Warranty.
>
> Seal: Ornate lys SIGILL' RANVLFI DUMPING.
>
> Early thirteenth century   AD L 2699

115. Robert f. Thoraldi de Salfletebi

> Quitclaims to Odo Galle and his heirs all his right in 40 acres in Saltfleetby, with the advowson of the church of St. Clement of Saltfleetby, which is situated in the aforesaid acres, touching which Alan the clerk Robert's brother, impleaded Odo by the king's writ. Odo has given Robert 40 shillings.
>
> Warranty.
>
> Sealing clause.
>
> Early thirteenth century   AD L 2843

116. Adam f. Roberti f. Moléé

> Grants to his brother Thoui and his heirs or assignees, all the meadow he had in Cucroft, all his right and claim in Micheldych, and all his share in Agmare, namely the third part. To hold of the lord of the fee

at a yearly rent of 3 pence. For this gift Thoui has given him 2 marks of silver.

Warranty.

Slit only for seal tag.

Early thirteenth century   AD L 2639

117. Wigot f. Asgeri

Grants to Walter Galle and his heirs a piece of land 2 perches in breadth, containing an acre and a half, in Saltfleetby, to hold of Wigot and his heirs at a yearly rent of $2\frac{1}{2}$ pence.

Seal: Lys SIGILLVM V. GOTI FILII ASGERI.

Circa 1180   *Danelaw Charters* no. 537

118. Hemming and Robert filii Willelmi Strawelaus et filii Quenilde filie Hemming de Salfletebi

Sell and quitclaim to Odo Galle and his heirs all the land which they held of him in Saltfleetby except $4\frac{1}{2}$ acres, being the message of Hemming Sprenting, their grandfather. Odo has given them 2 marks of silver and a quitclaim to Hemming and Robert and their assignees in religion of the $4\frac{1}{2}$ acres aforesaid.

Heirs' consent.

Seals: 1. Device developed from lys + SIGILL' ROB'TI FILII WILLELMI.

2. Male figure standing armed with a sword facing grotesque animal + SIGILL' HEMING FILII WILLELMI.

Late twelfth century   *Danelaw Charters* no. 540

Other charters which are connected with the present charter are printed as *Danelaw Charters* nos. 538 and 539, and discussed in the Introduction to that book, pp. cxxx–cxxxi.

119. Robert the priest f. Stepy

Grants to Maud and Alice, his sisters, a toft and 4 acres of arable in Saltfleetby, to hold for the term of their lives, rendering yearly to Alan, Robert's brother 8 pence *ad quatuor terminos firme socagie*. If Maud and Alice shall die in Robert's lifetime, this land shall revert to Robert, subject to the yearly rent of 8 pence to Alan. The latter will warrant the land to whomsoever Robert shall assign it.

Robert has confirmed this charter with his own seal and that of Alan.

One seal remains: + SIGILL' ALANI FILII STEPI.

Early thirteenth century   AD L 2597

120. Robert f. Stepi and Richard his brother

Grant to Andrew Galle and his heirs or assignees 16 acres in Saltfleetby. The grantees shall do to the lord of the fee the services due from this land.

Warranty.

Two seals: + SIGIL ROB FILII STEPI. + SIGILLVM . RIC' . FIL' . STEPI.

Circa 1220   AD L 2619

121. John f. Wigoht

     Grants to Walter son of Oda Galle 3 acres of meadow
     to hold of him at a yearly rent of 4½ pence.
     Warranty.
     Consent of John's brothers and heirs.
     Slit only for seal tag.
     Circa 1200   AD L 2532

122. Robert f. Wigoti

     Grants to Hodo Galle an acre of meadow to hold of
     him and his heirs at a yearly rent of 1 penny.
     Warranty.
     General heirs' consent.
     Seal: Cross with a dot in each angle SIGIL' ROBERTI
     . . . WIGOTI.
     Early thirteenth century   AD L 2762

123. Mabel widow of Robert f. Aylef

     Quitclaims to Odo Galle for half a mark of silver all
     her rights of dower in the lands which were Robert,
     her husband's, in Saltfleetby.
     Sealing clause.
     Early thirteenth century   AD L 2674

124. Maud f. Roberti f. Alyue de Saltfletebi

     Quitclaims to Thomas son of John of Louth and his
     heirs and assignees 10 acres in Saltfleetby. To hold at

a yearly rent of 16 pence to the Lord Abbot of Langonnet.

Heirs' consent.

Warranty.

Seal: Inverted lys SIGILL' MATILDIS FIL' ROB'.

Circa 1220   AD L 2778

125. Hawisia f. Robert f. Ayliue de Saltfletebi

Quitclaims, in her widowhood and free power, to Thomas son of John of Louth the 10 acres quitclaimed by Maud in the previous charter. To hold at a yearly rent of 16 pence to the abbot of Langonnet.

Warranty.

Sealing clause.

Seal: Inverted lys SIGILL' . AWISSE FIL' ROBER.

Circa 1220   AD L 2779

126. Mabel f. Aze de Yerthburch widow of Robert f. Ayliue de Saltfletebi

Quitclaims to Thomas son of John of Louth all her right in the land granted in the two preceding charters.

Sealing clause.

Affidatio in the hand of Osbert f. Helrici.

Seal: Inverted lys SIGILL' MABIL . FIL' AZE.

Circa 1220   AD L 2776

127. Hawisa f. Roberti f. Ailoue

(1) Grants, in her widowhood, to John son of Odo

Galle and his heirs 1 acre of meadow. To hold of her
and her heirs at a yearly rent of 2 pence. For this gift
John has given her 10 shillings.

Warranty.

Seal: SIGILLVM . . . FILIE ROBERTI.

Early thirteenth century   AD L 2579

128. Hawisa f. Roberti f. Ailoue

(2) Quitclaims, in her widowhood, to John son of
Odo Galle and his heirs all the lands which he has
from her or her family, namely 9 acres of the land of
Robert son of Ailiue in Saltfleetby. Rendering to her
and her heirs 2 pence from 1 acre in Saltfleetby and the
third part of an acre of meadow.

Warranty.

Seal, much defaced: Lys SIGIL . . .

Early thirteenth century   AD L 2589

129. Robert f. Radulfi f. Aldyth de Salfledeby

Quitclaims to Hugh son of Osbert of Saltfleetby and
his heirs his right in an acre and a half in Saltfleetby,
granted by his father Ralf to Hugh's father Osbert, at
a yearly rent of 5 pence 3 farthings to the lords of the
fee. For this gift Hugh has given Robert 2 marks.
Sealing clause.

Seal: Flower with six petals. SIGILL' ROBERTI FIL'
RAD.

Early thirteenth century   AD L 2666

130. Osbert f. Godiue

Grants to Odo Galle and his heirs 3 acres less half a perch in Apolcroft in Saltfleetby. To hold of the abbot of Langonnet at a yearly rent of 4 pence and 1 farthing.

Warranty.

Seal: Lys + SIGILL' OSBERTI F GODIVE.

Circa 1200   AD L 2536

131. William f. Geue de Salfleteby

Releases to Philip son of Odo Galle and his heirs a rent of 6 pence yearly which he used to pay William for land which he held of him in Saltfleetby. For this gift Philip has given William half a mark.

Sealing clause.

Seal.

Circa 1250   AD L 2787

132. William f. Jeue and John f. Me . . . de Salfleteby

Grant to Walter of Oxcumb and his heirs, assignees or legatees a croft of meadow in Saltfleetby which was Robert, son of Osbert son of Helric's. To hold of William and John and their heirs at a yearly rent of $3\frac{1}{2}$ pence.

Warranty.

Sealing clause.

Two seals: Ornate lys + S' WILL'I F' WALTERI.

Flower with eight petals SIL' : IOH'IS FIL' : WILL'.

1250–60   AD L 2614

Skidbrook

133. Askel f. Basing de Skitebroc

Grants to the commons of the church of Lincoln, in pure and perpetual alms, a toft in Skidbrook and the moiety of 4 selions there.

Consent of Alice, Askel's wife, and of his heirs.

Warranty.

Late twelfth century   Reg. Ant., f. 103b

134. Richard f. Asghari

Grants to the commons of the canons of Lincoln, in pure and perpetual alms, $4\frac{1}{2}$ acres in Fencropt and 3 other acres in Skidbrook, *scilicet tophtum et crophtum ubi sedit Ascerus filius Ougrimi.*

Circa 1180   D. & C. Linc. D ii. 87/1/19 [Now printed *Registrum Antiquissimum*, vol. v, no. 1767.]

135. Robert f. Sigward de Saltfleteby

Grants to the same 6 acres in Skidbrook.

Warranty.

Sealing clause.

Circa 1210   Reg. Ant., f. 101b

136. Hernis f. Haac Cnocting de Schitebroc

Grants to St. Mary and the chapter of Lincoln, in pure and perpetual alms, 3 acres and a perch in Esthaldecrof and Westhaldecrof.

Warranty.

Sealing clause.

Heirs' consent.

Circa 1200   D. & C. Linc. D ii. 87/1/12 [Now
   printed *Registrum Antiquissimum*, vol. v, no. 171b¹]
   A thirteenth-century endorsement to this charter
   names the grantor Ernis f. Acche Cnotting.

137. Hugh f. Wigoti f. Asgeri de Scitebroc

   Grants to the canons of Lincoln in pure and perpetual
   alms, an acre and a perch in Aicroft.

   Sealing clause.

   Circa 1210   Reg. Ant., f. 104b [Now printed *Regi-
                     strum Antiquissimum*, vol. v, no. 1720]

138. Godric f. Alnad

   Grants to the commons of the canons of Lincoln 3
   acres in Skidbrook.

   Warranty.

   Sealing clause.

   Cicra 1210   Reg. Ant., f. 105   [Now printed *ibid.*,
                                             vol. v, no. 1724]

¹ Several other charters granted by members of this family are printed
in vol. v of the *Registrum Antiquissimum*: e.g. an original charter by Hugh
Knotting granting half an acre in Skidbrook to the common of the canons
(no. 1715). As Hugh son of Wigot Chonoting the same man confirms a
grant to the common of the canons made by Roger son of Wigot of
Skidbrook (no. 1721) of half a salt meadow and adds to it the other
half (No. 1722). Beatrice widow of Wigot Chonoting quitclaims to
the common of the canons of Lincoln the 6 acres of land and the salt-pan
in Skidbrook which her sons Roger and Hugh gave them (*Registrum
Antiquissimum*, vol. v, no. 1723).

139. Robert f. Godrici

Grants to the same 2 acres in Skidbrook.
Warranty.
Sealing clause.
Circa 1210   Reg. Ant., f. 104 [Now printed *Registrum Antiquissimum*, vol. v, no. 1718]

140. Hugh f. Willelmi f. Adestani de Westorp in Schitebrok

Grants to Alvingham priory, in pure and perpetual alms, the half of a *fossatum* in Skidbrook.
Warranty.
Sealing clause.
Circa 1260   Laud MS. 642, f. 89

141. Boniua f. Basing de Blaikemare de Schitebroc

Grants to Odo Galle of Saltfleetby and his heirs 6½ acres of land to hold of her and her heirs at a yearly rent of 8 pence 3 farthings.
Warranty.
Circa 1200   Danelaw Charters no. 554

142. Gilbert f. Magni de Sumercotes

Grants to Boniua daughter of Ranulf of Somercotes and her heirs all his land by the sand hills (*apud meles*) in Skidbrook, to hold of Gilbert and his heirs at a yearly rent of one halfpenny. For this gift Boniua has given 12 pence to Gilbert.

Heirs' consent.

Warranty.

Seal.

Late twelfth century *Danelaw Charters* no. 555

143. Godric f. Uue de Schitebroc

Sells to Robert f. Willelmi le Norais a piece of land 20 feet in breadth at the south side of his toft, and a plot 20 feet in length by 10 in breadth within his toft on the south side to make a house. To hold of Godric at a yearly rent of 2 pence.

Warranty.

Seal.

Circa 1225 AD L 3019

144. Gilbert f. Brunnis de Thedelestorp

Quitclaims to Odo Galle and his heirs the land which Boniva f. Basinge, Gilbert's aunt, gave to Odo, whereof Gilbert had impleaded Odo at Lincoln by writ of mort d'ancestor before Alexander abbot of Peterborough, Martin of Pattishall, and their fellows, justices itinerant.

Consideration: 20 shillings.

Warranty.

Seal: SIGILL' GILB'TI FILII BRVNIS.

1222–6 AD L 2986

145. Hugh f. Brunnis de Thedelethorp

Quitclaims to the same the same land in Skidbrooke. Warranty.

Seal: SIGILL HVGONIS FIL BRVNIS.

1222–6   AD L 2987

146. Ralf f. Ernis f. Gille de Schitebroc

Party to *conventio* with Simon f. Willelmi of the same place. Ralf at his death will leave to Simon all the land which he holds of him by the sand hills (*ad meles*) if he has no heir by his wife. Simon or his heirs shall acquit Ralf or his assignees of their charges in respect of the house built on this land.

Warranty.

Small seal in bad condition.

Circa 1230   AD L 2947

147. David f. Swayn de Schitebroc

Grants to John his brother and his heirs a toft with the house built on it and 5 selions and a headland, to hold of the lord of the fee at a yearly rent of 4 pence *ad quatuor terminos in socka de Gaytun constitutos*. For this grant John has given 5 marks of silver to David.

Warranty.

Seal.

Circa 1240   AD L 2928

148. As David f. Schuynn' [*sic*] de Schittebroch'

Grants to Phillip Galle of Saltfleetby and his heirs 3½ acres of arable, rendering yearly 4 pence to the lord of the fee at the terms customary in the soke of Gayton, and 3 pence to Robert the miller.

Warranty.

Seal: s'DAVID FIL'I SVAIN.

Circa 1240   AD L 2945

149. Henry f. Johannis f. Prude de Schitebroch'

Grants to Phillip Galle the third part of 1 selion in the place called Wldhouhe, between the lands of Henry's brothers David and Gilbert on the north and south respectively, rendering to the lord of the fee the service due from the land.

Warranty.

Sealing clause.

Circa 1250   D. of L. Cart. Misc. II. 41/3

150. John f. Wluiue de Skitebroc

(1) Grants to William f. Ricardi, *persona* of the village, the moiety of the land *ad dunes* which John bought from Hugh f. Acke and Juliana his wife, to hold at a yearly rent of 1 farthing.

Warranty.

Circa 1250   AD L 2926

151. John f. Wluiue de Skitebroc

(2) Grants to Alice daughter of John of Saltfleetby a parcel of land 14 feet in length and 24 feet in breadth between John's land and le hutegang to hold at a yearly rent of 1 halfpenny.

Warranty.

Circa 1250   D. of L. Cart. Misc. III. 76/1

152. Richard f. Hutth'ii

Grants to Phillip Galle and his heirs half an acre of meadow, to hold of Richard and his heirs. For this grant Phillip has given half a mark to Richard.

Warranty.

Seal: s' RIC. OVTI.

Circa 1250   AD L 2990

153. Richard f. Asgeri

Grants to Odo Galle and his heirs 2 acres of arable, less 1 perch, to hold of Richard and his heirs at a yearly rent of 3 pence.

Warranty.

Circa 1220   D. of L. Cart. Misc. II. 6/4

154. Emma and Maud filie Hugonis filii Godrici

Release to Walter f. Agnetis de Schitebroc and Leuiue his wife all their right in the land of Hugh their father lying *ad dunes*.

Sealing clause, and two seals appended to the charter.

Circa 1250   AD L 2924

Somercotes

155. Arnegrim de Sumercotes

Grants to the nuns and brethren of Alvingham, in pure and perpetual alms, a close of meadow of 5 acres.

Consent of Robert, Arnegrim's son and heir.

Warranty.

Circa 1180   Laud MS. 642, f. 90

156. Osbert f. Gille de Grimolby et Derwen f. Gunne de Sumercotes sponsa eius et Robertus filius eorum

Grant to the same all their land in Somercotes, free from all service saving the right of the lords of that fee. They have made this gift and quitclaimed all their right in this land, together with Godfrey son of Osbert and Derwen, whom the nuns and brethren have received into their fellowship. They have given their right hands and pledged their faith to warrant the land to the nuns and brethren at the latter's charge.

Circa 1180   Ibid., f. 90b

157. William f. Alfesi de Sumercotes

Confirms to the same the site of their mill by the south green of Somercotes to hold in fee-farm of him and his heirs, the priory milling for them 10 *schepas* of corn yearly without payment.

Consent of wife and heirs.
Warranty.
Circa 1200   Ibid., f. 90

158. Robert f. Asceri de Sumercotes

   (1) Grants to the same, in pure and perpetual alms,
   a selion of arable.
   Warranty.
   Circa 1200   Ibid., f. 90b

159. Robert f. Asceri de Sumercotes

   (2) Re-grants to the same this selion, describing it as
   a perch of arable extending from a certain way
   towards the south until it contains a full perch of
   arable.
   Warranty.
   Circa 1200   Ibid.

160. Ernis and Robert filii Thorgoti de Nort Sumercotes

   Grant to the same, in pure and perpetual alms, an
   acre of meadow.
   Warranty.
   Circa 1220   Ibid.

       Sara, Ernis's widow, renounces whatever claims
       she has by reason of dower in the meadow which
       her husband sold to the priory. Ibid.

161. Richard f. Stepi de Sumercotes

Grants to the same, in pure and perpetual alms, an acre of meadow.

Warranty.

Circa 1210   Laud MS. 642, f. 90b

162. Tonna quondam uxor Ricardi f. Stepi

Confirms to the same the meadow of her husband's gift, and releases all her claim in it by reason of dower. Sealing clause.

Circa 1220   Ibid., f. 91

163. Asger f. Gunne de Sumercotes and his heirs

Grant to the nuns of Alvingham 10 acres of meadow at a yearly rent of 16 pence. Asger has confirmed this gift by pledging his faith in the hand of Geoffrey the priest.

Circa 1160   Ibid.

The attestations, which are omitted from the copy in the cartulary, were introduced by the phrase *Huius donacionis sunt fideiussores et testes*.

164. William f. Asgeri de Sumercotes

Confirms to the same the 10 acres of meadow given by his father. The priory shall render 16 pence yearly to William and his heirs.

Warranty.

Circa 1200   Ibid.

165. William f. Hugonis de Sumercotes and Geue filia Gunewat his aunt

Make an indented agreement recording the equal partition of their land in Somercotes, of whatever fee it is held. For a selion in Hauerdale and a rent of 2 pence from Hawis, Godric's wife, Geua and her heirs shall pay 2 pence a year to Richard f. Stepi, and 1 halfpenny a year to the heirs of Jungwin. For the rest, William and Geua shall pay in common the rents due from their lands to the lords of the fees of which they hold.

William and Geua have pledged their faith in the hand of William the clerk to observe this agreement. Seal: Oval, spray of symmetrical foliage, SIGILL GEVE FILIE GVNE.

Circa 1225   AD L 3097

166. Peter f. Aeilsi

Grants to the commons of the canons of Lincoln, in pure and perpetual alms, 2 acres and 1 perch of arable. Warranty.

Circa 1200   Reg. Ant., f. 96b [Now printed *Registrum Antiquissimum*, vol. v, no. 1663]

167. Auke de Somercotes

Grants to the same, in alms, $16\frac{1}{2}$ acres of arable and 7 acres of meadow.

General consent of heirs.

Warranty.
Sealing clause.
Circa 1210   Reg. Ant., f. 96b[1]

168. Godric f. Hemmig de Sumercotes

Grants to the chapter of Lincoln, in alms, 8½ acres in Sumercotes.

Consent of Hawisa, Godric's wife, and his heirs.

Warranty.

Sealing clause.

Circa 1200   Ibid., f. 99 [Now printed *Registrum Antiquissimum*, vol. v, no. 1682]

169. Hawis wife of Godric de Sumercotes

Releases to the same all her claim by reason of dower in the land which Alneth f. Hemmig holds of the chapter in Somercotes.

Sealing clause.

Circa 1200   Ibid., f. 99 [Now printed *Registrum Antiquissimum*, vol. v, no. 1683]

[1 See *Registrum Antiquissimum*, vol. v, no. 1675. No. 1693 is a grant by Rumfar son of Auke of Somercotes to the common of the canons of 4 acres of land in Somercotes. No. 1694 is a confirmation by William son of Auke of the preceding grant made by Rumfar his brother. No. 1695 is an acknowledgement by William that he holds 4 acres of land in Somercotes at a rent to the chapter of 18 pence, that he may not sell the land and the chapter will not warrant it to him.]

It may be assumed that this land is identical with that given by Godric f. Hemmig. Alneth the tenant will therefore be Godric's brother.

170. Basing f. Osgoti de Sumercotes

Grants to the commons of the canons of Lincoln, in pure and perpetual alms, 8½ acres of arable, *scilicet a A usque ad uiam uersus austrum.*
Warranty.
Sealing clause.

Circa 1210   Ibid., f. 96b [Now printed *Registrum Antiquissimum*, vol. v, no. 1665]

The 'A' of this charter is the dyke known at the present time as the Great Eau.

171. As Basing f. Hosgoti de Sumercotes

Grants to the same, in pure and perpetual alms, 2½ acres of land.
Warranty.
Sealing clause.

Circa 1210   Ibid., f. 96b [Now printed *Registrum Antiquissimum*, vol. v, no. 1664]

172. Gilbert f. Magnus de Sumercotes

Grants to God and St. Mary of Lincoln, in pure and

perpetual alms, 4 acres near the way called Hunder-fure.

Sealing clause.

Circa 1160 Reg. Ant., f. 99 [Now printed *Registrum Antiquissimum*, vol. v, no. 1681]

173. Wigot de Sumercotes.

Grants to the same 10 acres lying in five separate places.

Circa 1180 Ibid. f. 97

174. Robert f. Bonnif de Sumercothes.

Grants to Phillip Galle of Saltfleetby all the service, and 1 halfpenny of yearly rent, which he was accustomed to receive from Thomas Holebol *pro tribus fallis et dimidia iacentibus in crofto meo.*

Sealing clause.

Circa 1260 AD L 3194

Welton le Wold

175. Torold de Welletun

(1) Grants to the nuns of Ormsby, in pure and perpetual alms, 6 acres of his free socage on the east of Lofdale.

Warranty.

Consent of Torold's wife, of Walter his son, and of his other sons.

Circa 1170 Gilbertine Charters, p. 58

176. Turold de Welletuna

(2) Grants to Kirkstead abbey, in pure and perpetual alms, three parcels of land, each 3 perches broad, in Welton.

Consent of Aubrey, Turold's wife and of Walter his son and heir.

Turold and Walter have pledged their faith to observe this grant in the hand of Elias priest of Gayton le Wold.

Circa 1170   Cott. Vesp. E xviii, f. 88

177. Walter f. Thorold et Helis frater eius

Grant to Henry f. Ade de Witchal, chaplain, and his assignees four separate parcels of land in Welton, to hold in pure and perpetual alms, rendering yearly to the rectors of the church of Welton 1 halfpenny for the welfare of the souls of the grantors.

Warranty.

Two seals: 1. White wax, legend obliterated. 2. Green wax, S' HELIE FILII THORADI.

Circa 1225   AD L 3093

Walter son of Thorald made numerous other grants by charter, in particular to the vicars choral of Lincoln cathedral, in whose cartulary copies of these charters are preserved.

178. Osbert f. Hedus de Welletona

Grants to Phillip Galle de Saltfletby and his heirs 4

acres in Welton at a yearly rent of 1 halfpenny. For this grant Phillip has given 20 shillings to Osbert.

Warranty.

Sealing clause.

Circa 1250   AD L 3172

Seal: SIGILL' OSBER' FIL' EDIT.

> The legend on the seal proves that the forms Hedus, Edusa, Edus, which are not uncommon in the Danelaw, are pet forms of Edith.

179. William f. Willelmi f. Hamund de Velltona

Grants to the same 3 acres in Welton at a yearly rent of 1 penny. For this grant, Phillip has given 10 shillings to William.

Warranty.

Sealing clause.

Slit for seal tag.

Circa 1250   D. of L. Cart. Misc. I. 8/2

180. Edith filia Willelmi f. Lelle de Welletona

Releases in her widowhood to Henry the chaplain son of Adam of Withcall and his assignees all her claim by reason of dower in 2 acres which Thomas her husband granted to Henry.

Sealing clause.

Seal: SIGILL' HEDETH FIL WILELMI.

Circa 1225   AD L 3091

181. Robert f. Agemundi de Cotes

Grants to Kirkstead abbey, in pure and perpetual alms, a piece of land 3 perches in breadth in Welton. Warranty.

Robert has made this grant with the consent of John his son-in-law, so that John has confirmed it with his seal.

Circa 1160   Cott. Vesp. E xviii, f. 89

Yarburgh

182. Emma filia Suain de Jerburc

Grants to Alvingham priory, in pure and perpetual alms, the toft which was Gille's, 20 acres of arable on one side of the village of Yarburgh and 20 acres on the other, and 8 acres of meadow in the meadows of Yarburgh. Warranty.

Circa 1200   Laud MS. 642, f. 117b

Wraggoe Wapentake

Snelland

183. Suain Haribrun

In association with Helto of Snelland, Henry de Merula, Tomas the clerk, Jocelin the carpenter, and Simon his brother, quitclaims to the monks of Kirkstead a way lying between the toft of Richard Haribrun and the toft of Geoffrey f. Acche in exchange for a way which the monks have made over the toft which was Richard of Hoyland's.

Each of these men has pledged his faith to observe this transaction, and those who have seals have appended them.

Late twelfth century   Laud MS. 642, f. 119

Southrey

184. William f. Ivonis f. Scethman

Confirms to Bardney abbey the alms which his father gave, namely his whole fee in Southrey, in men and in essart, etc.

Consent of his mother and brothers.

William has given the church seisin by a knife offered upon the altar before his kinsfolk.

Circa 1150   Cott. Vesp. E xx, f. 86

Swinethorpe in Snelland

185. Symon f. Stainbid de Sunethorp

Grants to Kirkstead abbey, in pure and perpetual alms, 1 selion in the fields of Swinethorpe.

Warranty.

Late twelfth century   Cott. Vesp. E xviii, f. 122b

Torrington

186. Dolfin et Helewisa his sister

Are recorded to have granted to Bullington priory, with reservation of forensic service, a bovate in

Torrington which Roger f. Jocelini formerly gave to
Dolfin for his service.

In confirmation by Roger Mustela, *circa* 1165.

Harl. MS. 6118, p. 39 f.

KESTEVEN

Aswardhurn Wapentake

Ewerby

187. William f. Ulf de Ywarbi et Jacob filius eius

Grant to Haverholme priory 10½ acres of meadow of
their demesne in exchange for the land and wood
which Ulf, William's father, had formerly given. They
also grant to the same the marsh called Otresholm,
being 10 acres.

Circa 1155

Lincolnshire Notes & Queries, vol. xvii, p. 22

Beltisloe Wapentake

Bitchfield

188. William f. Algeri

Is recorded to have granted to Vaudey abbey 20 acres
in the wood called Collehage in Bitchfield.

In confirmation by Richard I.   Mon. Ang. v. 490

Bulby

189. Richard f. Gamel de Bolebi

Grants in marriage with Alice, his daughter, to Richard of Morton and the heirs or assignees of Alice and

Richard 10 selions of his land in Bulby. To hold of Richard son of Gamel and his heirs at a yearly rent of 1 penny.

Warranty.

Sealing clause.

Mid-thirteenth century   Add. Chart. 20647

190. Maud filia Thome and Thomas her son

Quitclaim to the nuns of Sempringham, in pure and perpetual alms, the whole fee and tenement of Osbert f. Colgrimi, Maud's grandfather, in Bulby. They also confirm the gift of this tenement made by Nigel son of Alexander.

Seal.

Circa 1180–90   Add. Chart. 20625

191. John f. Hasti de Bolebi

Grants to Sempringham priory, in pure and perpetual alms, half a bovate and 2 acres which his father acquired at law against Robert of Langton.

Consent of Godfrey and William, John's brothers.

Warranty.

Seal: Bird SIGILLV HANCLARE.

Late twelfth century   Danelaw Charters no. 435
    There is also extant another grant of the same land by Geoffrey f. Asketini de Bolebi. The Asketin of this charter is identical with the Hasti of the charter which has just been described (ibid. no. 436).

Edenham

192. Hugh f. Gillæ

Is recorded to have granted to Vaudey abbey 9 acres, 1 rood, apparently of arable, and meadow in Edenham. In confirmation by Richard I.   Mon. Ang. v. 490

Hawthorpe

193. Ralf f. Spracli de Hawrtorp et Willelmus frater eius

Grant to the nuns of Sempringham, in perpetual alms, 17 acres of their land in Hawthorpe and common of pasture in that village, as much as belongs to their fee. They will acquit this land from all gelds and aids and customs.

Consent of Robert of Langton their lord and of their brothers and heirs.

Warranty.

Affidatio in the hand of Gocelin the priest.

Consideration: 4 marks.

Circa 1160   Danelaw Charters no. 438

Boothby Wapentake

Boothby Graffoe

194. Walter f. Agge de Boby

Grants to Reginald son of Alan, his heirs and assignees 1 acre, and 1 rood, and 2 furrows of arable in Bothby. To hold of Walter and his heirs at a yearly rent of 1 penny.

Warranty.
Sealing clause.
Circa 1260   Cott. Faustina B i, f. 47

Navenby (Nauenby)

195. Robert nepos Agge

Grants to the *communa* of the canons of Lincoln, in
pure and perpetual alms, a parcel of land which he
held of Anselin de Waten.
Warranty.
Sealing clause.
Early thirteenth century

D. & C. Linc. D ii. 89/3/46

196. Gilbert f. Quenild

Grants to the same a similar parcel of land.
Warranty.
Sealing clause.
Early thirteenth century   Ibid. 89/3/45

Flaxwell Wapentake

Rauceby

197. Adam f. Lewini de Rouceby

Grants to William his brother 2 of the 3 bovates
which William son of Agnes formerly held in Rauceby
and the toft which was formerly Ivete, Hugh the
clerk's sister's. To hold to William and his heirs of
Adam and his heirs, with all the appurtenances except

the tofts and crofts belonging to those bovates, at a yearly rent of 3 shillings and 2 pence.

Warranty.

Sealing clause.

Mid thirteenth century

Aug. Off. Misc. Bks. 48/250

Langoe Wapentake

Blankney

198. Robert f. Roberti f. Hulf de Methringham

Grants to Kirkstead abbey, in free, pure, and perpetual alms, a piece of meadow in Blankney.

Warranty.

Sealing clause.

Mid thirteenth century   Cott. Vesp. E xviii, f. 38

Branston

199. Thomas f. Suani

Grants to Kirkstead abbey, in alms, an acre in Branston of Osbert of Hanworth's fee, to which Thomas formerly laid claim, and half an acre in the same fields of Fulk del Alnei's fee.

Circa 1180–90   Ibid., f. 49

Thomas was probably brother of Roger son of Suan, who is known to have been a free tenant of John de Aincurt in 1169 (ibid., ff. 47–9).

Potter Hanworth

200. Roger f. Haconis

Grants to Richard his son 3 bovates and 2 tofts, which Orgar of Lincoln formerly held, and 1 bovate which Robert, Roger's brother, holds for the term of his life. To hold at a yearly rent of 10 shillings to Philip de Martona in lieu of all services other than that due to the king.

Sealing clause.

Early thirteenth century

Thurgarton Cartulary, f. 94

Scopwick

201. Deuleward f. Arketil

Grants to Thurgarton priory in free, pure, and perpetual alms half an acre of arable and four furrows.

Warranty.

Sealing clause.

Circa 1225   Ibid., f. 115

202. As Deuleward f. Arkel

Grants to Hervey le Neucomen de Scaupewic half an acre of arable in the territory of Scopwick and Kirkby Green, to hold of Deuleward and his heirs at a yearly rent of 1 halfpenny.

Consent of wife and heirs.

Warranty.

Sealing clause.

Circa 1225   Ibid., f. 123

203. Geoffrey f. Herewardi

Grants to Walter the clerk his son 1 acre of arable on each side of the village, at a yearly rent of 1 halfpenny. Warranty.

Circa 1225   Ibid., f. 118

204. Roger f. Wluiue de Kirkeby

Releases to William the prior and the monastery of Thurgarton all his right in 3½ bovates of meadow *extra Riskefen* which he had granted to them for the term of 12 years in the 26th year of the reign of King Henry son of King John. Roger promises to warrant this meadow and all the lands which they have of his gift in Kirkby Green and Scopwick before the king's justices.

Circa 1254   Ibid., f. 109b

205. Roger f. Swayn de Blankeney

Grants to the church of Holy Cross of Kirkby Green in free, pure, and perpetual alms all his meadow in the marsh between Kirkby and Scopwick, so that Robert the dean shall hold it of the church at a yearly rent of 1 halfpenny. Robert may grant this meadow to whomsoever he will, to hold of the church at the aforesaid rent.

Warranty.

Circa 1250   Ibid., f. 114b

206. Simon cappellanus f. Willelmi f. Lundi de Scaupewic

Releases to Amabilis his sister and Robert de Roues-
tona her husband and their heirs all his right in half
a toft with half a croft, 1 acre of arable, and a rent of
2 pence halfpenny in Scopwick and Kirkby Green.
Robert and Amabilis shall render 4 pence yearly to
Thurgarton priory, and 1 penny to the church of
St. Andrew of Scopwick to buy wax.
Sealing clause.

Circa 1250   Thurgarton Cartulary, f. 128b

Ness Wapentake

Thurlby

207. Geoffrey f. Leuerici de Brun

Grants to the nuns of St. Michael's Stamford, 8 acres,
apparently in Thurlby, in exchange for land formerly
given him by the nuns. If he shall be unable to warrant
these acres to the nuns they shall receive again the
land which they formerly gave him.

Late twelfth century   Madox Formulare no. 258

Uffington

208. William f. Gamelli de Hufingtona

Sells to Henry son of Gamell, his brother, 3 roods of
arable in the fields of Uffington. To hold to Henry,
his heirs or assignees, of William and his heirs at a
rent of 1 halfpenny yearly.
Consideration: 10 shillings.

Warranty.

Sealing clause.

Mid thirteenth century

Aug. Off. Misc. Bks. 49/126

Threo Wapentake

Honington

209. Alan the dyer of Lincoln et Robert f. Colgrimi

Quitclaim to Stixwould priory 7 selions on the north of Colgrim's toft touching which the convent impleaded them by the king's writ to hold of them at a yearly rent of 4 pence.

Warranty.

Alan and Robert have made this quitclaim before the knights in the 10 wapentakes at Ancaster.

Two seals: (1) lys . . . ANI TINCT . . .; (2) floriate lys . . . COLGRIMI.

Late twelfth century   Danelaw Charters no. 384

210. Hamo de Hundingtona f. Toli

Quitclaims to the same a bovate which his father bought of the Countess Lucy. He also releases after his death 7 selions which the Countess held of his father *in warnad'* (*sic*) for 4 pence yearly.

Circa 1160   Bod. Lib. Stixwould Charters 4

Welby

211. John f. Ingebr . . .

Is recorded to have granted to Vaudey abbey certain

unspecified portions of land with common of pasture over all his land in Welby.

In confirmation by Richard I.   Mon. Ang. V 491
The imperfect Ingebr . . . can hardly represent any other name than Ingebrand.

212. Robert Spron and John his son, Alan the clerk, Fegge, William f. Osberti.

Are recorded to have granted to the same other parcels of land in the same place.

In the same charter (ibid.).

Winnibriggs Wapentake

Casthorpe in Barrowby

213. Thomas f. Alfgarii

Is recorded to have granted to Swineshead abbey 6 bovates in Casthorpe.

In confirmation by Henry II.   Mon. Ang. V 337

HOLLAND

Elloe Wapentake

Lutton

214. William f. Thori and Simon f. Guidonis

Are recorded to have granted to Castle Acre priory 1 acre, apparently in Lutton. In confirmation by Gerard de Camville of all the land held by the monks in Sutton and Lutton in the year 1186.

Harl. MS. 2110, f. 71

Pinchbeck

215. Agge f. Siolfe (*sic*) de Pincebec

Grants to Siwat f. Eudonis de Spalding and his heirs a close lying between two royal ways in Pinchbeck. To hold of God and the altar of the church of St. Mary of Pinchbeck at a yearly rent of 1 penny in lieu of all service.

Heirs' consent.

Warranty.

Circa 1215   Harl. MS. 742, f. 165b

216. As Agge f. Siolf

Confirms the gift made by Hugh de Bradehus to the almonry of Spalding of the land which Lambert sellarius held of him. Agge also releases the rent of 2 pence which Hugh ought to render yearly for this land.

Sealing clause.

Circa 1215   Ibid., f. 327

217. Nigel f. Siolf

Grants to the almonry of Spalding, free from all service, three cottages (*bordellos*) with their adjacent gardens, two held by Simon Billere and one by Emelot. Nigel also grants a messuage of 20 feet in breadth with an adjacent garden of 31 feet in breadth.

Warranty.

Circa 1215   Ibid., f. 326 b

218. Ailric f. Aslac

Grants to the almonry of Spalding, in free, pure, and perpetual alms, 2 acres, so that Alfred the shepherd and his heirs shall hold them of the aforesaid almonry at a yearly rent of 16 pence.

Warranty to the almonry and to Alfred.

Circa 1200   Harl. MS. 742, f. 326

219. Arnald f. Toui

Grants to the almonry of Spalding, in free, pure, and perpetual alms, a parcel of land lying within defined boundaries in Pinchbeck.

Warranty.

Circa 1215   Ibid., f. 328b

220. Richard f. Grimketil Fod

Assents to the agreement made between Gilbert f. Lamberti and the almonry of Spalding, concerning the land which Richard's father held of Gilbert. Richard shall hold the aforesaid land of the almonry at a yearly rent of 6 shillings, continuing also the payment of 1 penny which his father Grimketil used to make to Gilbert for forinsec service.

Sealing clause.

Circa 1225   Ibid., f. 328b

Long Sutton

221. Richard f. Ulf de Sutton in Hoylond

Grants to the church of St. Mary of Sutton, in free,

pure, and perpetual alms, half an acre in the land newly reclaimed from the marsh, so that Simon f. Radulfi f. Almarii, sergeant (*serviens*) of Sutton, his heirs or assignees, shall hold it of the aforesaid church at a yearly rent of 1 penny to provide oil for one lamp burning before the cross within the church.

Circa 1220   Harl. MS. 2110, f. 73

Kirton Wapentake

Bicker

222. **Robert f. Girz de Bicra**

Is recorded to have granted to Swineshead abbey a toft, the quarter of his meadow in Hasfordhirne, 2 little selions, and a *cultura* near Wigtoft.

In confirmation by Henry II, *circa* 1170.

Mon. Ang. V. 337

223. **Gerdus**

Is recorded to have granted to Vaudey abbey a salt-pan in Bicker.

In confirmation by Richard I.   Ibid. V. 490

Presumably the 'Gerd' who made this gift was father of the Robert filius Girz of the previous entry. The name seems to represent ON Gyrðr, which is rarely found in England after the Conquest.

224. **Robert f. Toly de Bicra**

Grants to Thomas his brother and his heirs Gyppe-toft in return for the messuage which was their

father's. Thomas has granted the latter messuage to Robert in return for Gyppetoft.
Warranty.
Circa 1190   Reg. Ebor. II, f. 403

225. Thomas f. Tholi f. Sumerdi de Bicra
Grants to God, St. Mary, and St. John the Baptist *de Novo Loco* in Boston a croft of his land called Gyppe-croft in Bicker with the buildings set on it, to hold in pure and perpetual alms.
Warranty.
Circa 1200   Ibid., f. 403

Surfleet

226. Hugh f. Grimketil
Grants to John f. Godefridi de Surflet' the quarter of a bovate in Totetoft, to hold of Hugh and his heirs at a yearly rent of 1 halfpenny.
Warranty.
Circa 1200   Harl. MS. 742, f. 183

Titton

227. Swan f. God' de Wybertona
Grants to John f. Jordani de Sancto Botulpho 1 selion *in Braac de Tittona in Northschifting'* to hold of Swan and his heirs at a yearly rent of 2 pence.
Warranty.
Circa 1225   Reg. Ebor. II, f. 398

Skirbeck Wapentake

Freiston

228. Turold f. Toli de Halketoft

Grants to Kirkstead abbey, in perpetual alms, all the land which he or his father had in Windesland.

Warranty.

Large Seal: 8 petalled flower, damaged.

Circa 1180   *Danelaw Charters* no. 160

Leverton

229. Reginald f. Gilleberti f. Iust de Leuertune

Grants to the church of Holy Cross of Waltham, in free and perpetual alms, a close in Wlmeresty called Dunchecroft, to hold of Reginald and his heirs at a yearly rent of 12 pence.

Warranty.

Circa 1225   Cott. Tib. C ix, f. 114

230. John f. Ailwardi de Leuertune

Grants to the same church of Holy Cross of Waltham, in pure and perpetual alms, certain parcels of land, and certain rents in Leverton.

Warranty.

Sealing clause.

Circa 1225   Ibid.

231. As John f. Alward' de Leuerton'

Grants to the same in free, pure, and perpetual alms, 4 selions in Leverton.

Warranty.

Circa 1225   Ibid., f. 115

Skirbeck

232. William f. Agge de Skyrebec

Grants to Ringolf f. Brictmerii de Scyrebec half an acre in Estereneucroft to hold of William and his heirs at a yearly rent of 2 pence.

Warranty.

Circa 1210   Reg. Ebor. II, f. 402

233. Swan f. Siwatt' de Scyrebec

Grants to John f. Jordani de Sancto Botulpho all his meadow in Folcringtoft being so much as belongs to 8 bovates of land in that place, to hold of Swan and his heirs at a yearly rent of 2 pence.

Warranty.

Circa 1220   Ibid., f. 394b

234. Ralf and Alan filii Swan' de Skirbec'

Release to the abbey of St. Mary, York, all their right in the meadow which John f. Jordani had by gift of their father Swan in Folkertoft.

Sealing clause.

Circa 1230   Ibid., f. 402b

235. Aifleta f. Galfridi f. Lelle de Scyrebec

Grants to John f. Jordani a croft in Skirbeck called Neuland, being all the land which Rannulf de Scirebec and Edyua the grantor's sister held in Skirbeck of the fee of Ralf son of Stephen de Hoyland. To hold in

chief of Ralf de Hoyland at a yearly rent of 6 pence.
Warranty.

Circa 1220   Ibid., f. 401

236. John f. Eilfled f. Galfridi f. Lelle de Schirbec'

Confirms to John f. Jordani the croft which formed the
subject of the previous grant.

Circa 1230   Ibid., f. 401b

Wrangle

237. Thoregot de Wlmeresti

Grants to the church of Holy Cross of Waltham, in
pure and perpetual alms, all the land which he has in
the new close outside the close of Ralf f. Ernaldi.
Consent of Magnus, Thoregot's son and heir.
Warranty.

Circa 1200   Cott. MS. Tib. C ix, f. 108b

238. Eudo f. Toue

Grants to the same, in pure and perpetual alms, 5
perches of his *deila in deilis de Wrengl'*.
Warranty.

Circa 1200   Ibid., f. 106

239. Richard f. Houk'

Grants to the same, in pure and perpetual alms, for
the spiritual welfare of his lords, Hugh de Pessi and
Simon Brito, 4 acres of arable which he held of Hugh
de Pessi. By the advice of the Abbot of Waltham

Richard has charged his remaining land, which he has reclaimed from the sea, and a salt-pan, with the rent which he owes to Hugh, namely 18 pence, and 2 *sextaria* of salt.

Sealing clause.

Circa 1200   Cott. MS. Tib. C ix, f. 107b

By a charter of *circa* 1180 Richard de Pissi grants to Richard f. Ouk' all the land which the latter's father Houk' (*sic*) held of him in Wrangle, namely 4 acres and a salt-pan, at a yearly rent of 18 pence and 2 *sextaria* of salt (ibid.).

240. As Richard f. Oukes de Wrengl'

Grants to Kirkstead abbey, in free, pure, and perpetual alms, all his meadow in the meadows of Wrangle.

Warranty.

Circa 1200   Cott. Vesp. E xviii, f. 187b

241. Gunwat f. Herlewin'

Grants to the church of Holy Cross of Waltham, in pure and perpetual alms, all his land *ad Siwatmures* and *in Reddeiles*.

Warranty.

Circa 1220   Cott. Tib. C ix, f. 107

242. Gunnewat f. Jordani

Grants to the same, in pure and perpetual alms, all his meadow in Fencroft.

Warranty.

Circa 1220   Ibid., f. 113b

243. As Gunewat f. Jordani de Wrengl'

For the soul of William his brother grants to Kirkstead abbey, in free, pure, and perpetual alms, all his land within defined boundaries *in riscis de Wrengl'*.

Warranty.

Circa 1220   Cott. Vesp. E xviii, f. 186b

By another charter on the same folio Alan f. Gune-wati f. Jordani and Simon f. William f. Jordani confirm the above gift.

244. Richard f. Gunewati de Wrengl'

Grants to the same, in free, pure, and perpetual alms, a parcel of land in Wrangle, $6\frac{1}{2}$ perches in length and 4 perches in breadth, according to the perch of 18 feet.

Warranty.

Circa 1225   Ibid., f. 186

245. Houkes f. Roberti

Quitclaims to the church of Holy Cross of Waltham 2 acres in Wrangle.

Sealing clause.

Circa 1240   Cott. Tib. C ix, f. 113b

246. Walter f. Bele de Wrengl'

Grants to Kirkstead abbey, in free, pure, and perpetual alms, 4 perches of meadow in Netherhenges in Wrangle.

Warranty.

Circa 1220   Cott. Vesp. E xviii, f. 185b

247. Magnus f. Ywini

Grants to the same, in free and pure alms, a house which Simon Goldstan sold him.

Warranty.

Circa 1225   Cott. Vesp. E xviii, f. 185b

248. John f. Oukes de Wrengl'

Grants to the same, in free, pure, and perpetual alms, a parcel of land 14 perches in breadth according to the perch of 20 feet.

Warranty.

Circa 1230   Ibid., f. 187b

249. John the deacon f. Ouky de Wrengl'

Grants to the same, in free, pure, and perpetual alms, a parcel of land *in Huuerhenges de Wrengl'*.

Warranty.

Circa 1230   Ibid., f. 188

     The grantor of this charter is probably identical with John f. Oukes of the previous document.

250. Roger f. Haldani

Releases to the same all his right in the toft and *area* in Wrangle which Richard Hauk, *his antecessor*, formerly held of Gilbert of Benniworth.

Sealing clause.

Circa 1260   Ibid., f. 189

     The Richard Hauk to whom Roger refers is

probably identical with the man who appears in earlier documents as Richard f. Oukes and Richard f. Houk'.

251. Richard f. Swyft de Wrangel

Releases to the lady Hawysa de Quenci, Countess of Lincoln, the yearly rent of 1 halfpenny which the Countess owed him for certain land which she had by the grant of Adam f. Reginaldi f. Mathei *in riscis de Wrangela*.

Sealing clause.

Seal: SIGILL RIC FIL SWIFT.

Circa 1235   AD L 2460

NOTTINGHAMSHIRE

Bassetlaw Wapentake

Barnby Moor

252. Thori de Barnebi

Grants to Blyth priory 4 *percatae* of his land in Barnby, to hold of him and his heirs at a yearly rent of 4 pence.

Consideration: 4 shillings.

Warranty.

Late twelfth century   Harl. MS. 3759, f. 92

Beckingham

253. Walter f. Gamel de Bekyngham

Grants to Adam son of Simon the quarter of an acre in

Walter's toft, on the east of his house, to hold of him
and his heirs at a yearly rent of 1 penny.
Warranty.
Mid thirteenth century   Harl. MS. 3640, f. 96b

Adam son of Simon granted this quarter acre to
Adam son of Grimkel at a yearly rent of 12 pence
*ad quatuor terminos scilicet in quibus firma domini arch-
iepiscopi reddita est.* Adam son of Simon afterwards
granted this rent, with Adam son of Grimkel's
homage, to Welbeck abbey, charging it with a
yearly payment of 1 penny to himself (ibid.).

Blyth

254. Henry Paste f. Haconis bubulci

Grants to Blyth priory, in perpetual alms, three tofts
in Blyth which Hardulf had, to hold of Henry and his
heirs at a yearly rent of 12 pence.
Consideration: 30 shillings and a cow.
Warranty.
Henry, Gode his mother, Robert his brother, and
Aldus his sister, have sworn to observe this gift.
Circa 1180–90   Harl. MS. 3759, f. 54

255. Johannes f. Jori quondam de Blida

Quitclaims to William de Leyrtona *cissor*, his kinsman,
all his right in the toft which was formerly Jori, John's
father's, in Blyth.

Consideration: 2 marks.
Sealing clause (incomplete).
Circa 1220–30   Ibid., f. 63

Eakring

256. Robert f. Scakel and Herbert his brother

Grant to Rufford abbey 5 acres and 1 rood in Eakring in perpetual alms. They also quitclaim the bovate in Rufford which Ougrim their uncle held and Robert his son and heir gave in alms when he became a monk.

Warranty of the land in Eakring.

Affidatio in the hand of William *monachi de Seympol*.

Because Robert and Herbert have no seal they have appended that of William de Tulc.

Circa 1180–90   Danelaw Charters no. 350

257. Wlsi f. Wlf de Eicringe

Surrenders and quitclaims to the monks of Rufford 3 acres of arable which he held of them. These acres were of demesne of Walter de Gant and Earl Gilbert de Gant his son, belonging to that part of the demesne of Rufford which the monks hold. The monks shall keep Godguin his son in their house until he comes to full age. If he then wishes to become a lay brother, the monks shall receive him *in ordine conuersorum*; if not, the aforesaid land shall still remain to the monks in alms.

Affidatio in the hand of Robert de Runchover.

Because Wlsi has no seal he has caused that of Adam parson of Eakring to be appended to this charter.

Circa 1150   B.M. Facsimiles no. 48

258. William f. Roberti f. Arkilly de Eykring

Confirms to the monks of Rufford the acre in Eakring which his father gave them in alms. He also adds another acre of his own gift in pure and perpetual alms.

Circa 1200–20   Harl. MS. 1063, f. 21b

259. Gilbert de Schegebi

Party to *conventio* with the monks of Rufford by which he grants them in perpetual alms, 10 acres which his father held of William de Albani in Eakring. They shall pay him 8 pence yearly, but shall be quit of this rent after his death.

Consideration: A mare and its foal. An ill-copied clause which follows apparently means that the monks shall receive his body for burial.

Circa 1160   Ibid., f. 10

By a charter entered on the same folio of the cartulary William de Albani grants 10 acres in Lactune hagri in Eakring to Gilbert and William sons of Wulsi at a yearly rent of 13 pence. Another charter of Gilbert of Skegby describes the 10 acres which he gave to Rufford as lying in Lactunhage. Gilbert of

Skegby may therefore be identified with Gilbert son of Wulsi. The latter is probably identical with Wulsi son of Wulf of Eakring whose charter to Rufford has been described above (no. 257).

Hodsock

260. Geoffrey f. Ricardi de Hodesac

Party to *conuencio* with R. de Pauliaco, the prior, and the convent of Blyth. Geoffrey confirms to the prior and monks, in pure and perpetual alms, the land, namely 3 acres between Blyth and Woodhouse, which Wlmer his grandfather gave to the monastery and Richard his father held of the same at rent for 6 pence yearly. He also confirms the moiety of the meadow called Fliccesheng which Richard his father gave to the monastery. The prior and convent grant this land to Geoffrey to hold of them for 18 pence yearly, upon condition that if he cannot hold the land and meadow with the aid of the prior and monks he shall nevertheless pay the aforesaid alms of 18 pence a year.

24 July 1188, in the monastery of Blyth

Harl. MS. 3759, f. 100

Morton by Retford

261. Walter f. Leuenat de Mortona

Grants to Rufford abbey, in perpetual alms, all his

land of Morton, free from all service except that due to the king and to Walter's lords of Bothamsall.

Consideration: 20 shillings.

Walter shall warrant this land as his own (*sicut proprium ius meum*) against all men except my lords of Bothamsall.

Affidatio in the hand of Hugh Folenfant.

Because Walter has no seal he has appended that of Hugh Folenfant.

Late twelfth century   Danelaw Charters no. 369

262. Roger f. Leuenat de Mortona

Grants to Rufford abbey, in pure and perpetual alms, all his land of Morton, free from all service due to the king and to Roger's lords of Bothamsall. The gift is to take effect after his death. He also grants in pure and perpetual alms, two portions of his land, one near the monks' orchard, the other a headland at the head of a *cultura* of the monks. These gifts are to take effect in Roger's lifetime.

Consent of Emma, Roger's wife.

Because Roger has no seal he has sealed this charter with his wife's key.

Late twelfth century   Ibid., no. 370

South Leverton

263. Robert f. Ade f. Grim de Sutheleuertona

Grants to John son of Henry of Cotum a headland in South Leverton in exchange for a selion there.

Warranty.

Sealing clause.

Circa 1260

> D. and C. Linc. Cartae Decani no. 176, f. 64b

Bingham Wapentake

Flintham

264. Alexander f. Swani de Aslactona

Grants to Welbeck abbey, in free, pure, and perpetual alms, an acre and half a rood of arable of the fee of Lancaster in Flintham, to hold of him and his heirs. Consent of Alice, Alexander's wife, and his heirs. Warranty.

Circa 1200   Harl. MS. 3640, f. 112

Kneeton

265. Ralf f. Willalmi f. Swani de Kniuetona

Grants to Welbeck abbey, in free, pure, and perpetual alms, 1 acre of arable in Kneeton. Warranty.

Sealing clause.

Mid thirteenth century   Ibid., f. 85b

Broxtow Wapentake

Watnall (Watinhow)

266. Hugh f. Chaskini de Brocbresting

Grants to Peter his son the moiety of the land which

he holds of Roger de Ridingis in Watnall, to hold at a yearly rent of 3 shillings and 8 pence to Roger. Sealing clause and slit for seal tag.

Early thirteenth century   AD B 6188

Rushcliffe Wapentake

Costock

267. Azur de Notingham

Grants to Garendon abbey 4 bovates in Cortingest' which he holds by hereditary right of William son of Wulfric. The monks shall hold the land free and quit of all service for 2 shillings yearly.

Circa 1150   Lansd. MS. 415, f. 17

268. Matthew f. Willelmi f. Wlurici

Confirms to the same, in perpetual alms, the 4 bovates in Costock which William his father gave to the monks free and quit of all service except 2 shillings. He now releases those 2 shillings, and upon his death the monks shall do for him as for a monk of their house. He also notifies that they owe no forinsec service for this land except $3\frac{1}{2}$ pence to Danegeld, which they shall pay to him and his heirs.

Warranty.

Circa 1160   Ibid., f. 16b

Thurgarton Wapentake

Carlton near Gedling

269. Hugh f. Aldredi

Grants to the canons of Thurgarton, in pure and perpetual alms, the toft and croft which were Anki's and 1 bovate which Robert the clerk held. Hugh's heirs will acquit this land from all service.

Warranty.

Circa 1180–90

Southwell Cathedral, Thurgarton Cartulary, f. 61b

This gift is confirmed by Robert f. Hugonis f. Aldredi de Carletona and by William f. Hugonis f. Aldredi.

Fiskerton

270. Blacman et Wolsi de Mortona

Are recorded in a confirmation by Robert son of Ralf of Fiskerton, to have given to the canons of Thurgarton, in return for their fraternity, 1 selion in Fiskerton.

Late twelfth century   Ibid., f. 10b

Kelham

271. William clericus et Ralf f. Roberti et Robert f. Botilde et Gilbert f. Willelmi

Grant to Rufford abbey, in perpetual alms 4 bovates which they held in Kelham. The monks shall give to Ralf of Hockerton 16 pence yearly for this land, which Geoffrey of Staunton gave them in perpetual alms. Notified by the chapter of Southwell under their seal.

Circa 1150–60   Danelaw Charters no. 358

272. Richard f. Roberti f. Anke de Kelum

Grants to Rufford abbey, in pure and perpetual alms, 5 acres, being 9 selions and a gore, to the north of the deep way called Sumergate, also 1 rood in the south field of Kelham.

Warranty.

Early thirteenth century   Harl. MS. 1063, f. 47b

273. William f. Goduini de Newerc

Confirms to Rufford Abbey all the meadow in the meadow of Kelham which Walter the chaplain, his uncle, gave, namely the meadow belonging to the 3 bovates which Henry son of William of Kelham holds. To hold of William and his heirs, in pure and perpetual alms as Walter's charter bears witness.

Tag for seal.

Early thirteenth century   Harl. Chart. 84 A 4

274. Suan f. Roberti de Kelum and Richard his brother

Grant to the monks of Rufford in perpetual alms, all the land, tilled and untilled, which they or their ancestors had in *fructetis et haithes* in the territory of Kelham.

Consideration: 2 cows in calf and 8 lambs.

Warranty.

Because Suan and Richard have no seal they have caused that of Hugh de Bulli to be appended to this charter.

Circa 1200   Harl. MS. 1063, f. 48b

Suan and Richard sons of Robert were probably grandsons of Anke of Kelham (above). Their charter is attested by Simon son of Anke. By two other charters in the cartulary Richard son of Robert granted respectively 5 roods and half an acre to the abbey.

275. Walter the chaplain of Coddington f. Willelmi f. Wlnet de Newerc

Grants to the monks of Rufford all his meadow belonging to the 3 bovates which Henry son of William of Kelham holds of him in the latter place, to hold of him and his heirs, in pure and perpetual alms.

Warranty.

Circa 1220–30   Harl. MS. 1063, f. 71

Thurgarton

276. Roger f. Suani

Grants to the canons of Thurgarton, in pure and perpetual alms, a toft in Thurgarton which Agnes, Manfrid's daughter, holds of the canons, and a bovate in the fields of the village.

Consent of wife and heirs.

Circa 1160

Southwell Cathedral, Thurgarton Cartulary, f. 2

DERBYSHIRE

Appletree Wapentake

Bradley

277. Orm de Cornl'

Grants to Alexander de Rames' 3 acres in Northfeld' which stretch from Attelouwerug' to Chedleker, to hold of Orm and his heirs at a yearly rent of 6 pence. Warranty.

Sealing clause.

Circa 1250   D. & C. Linc. Kniveton Leiger, f. 33

Hognaston

278. William f. Roberti f. Leuerici de Hokenaston

Grants to Peter f. Radulfi de Gratton' half a bovate in Hognaston which Engenulf f. Roberti de Combrugge formerly held, to hold of William and his heirs at a yearly rent of 4 pence for the term of 12 years from the date of the charter.

Warranty.

Sealing clause.

1268   Ibid., f. 73b

Thurvaston

279. Robert f. Nicholli

Grants to Tutbury priory, in perpetual alms, 40
acres in Turwardistona, 35 of them being arable and
5 meadow, with all the rights of common which
existed in that village in the time of Dolfin, Robert's
grandfather, and Nicholas, his father. Robert also
grants to the same 2 bovates in the same village.
Circa 1160   Add. MS. 6714, p. 58

High Peak Wapentake

Brushfield

280. Walthef de Morneshale

Is known to have made various agreements with
Rufford abbey by which the abbey became possessed
of a portion of the fee which Walthef held in Brushfield in this wapentake of Sewale f. Fulcheri. A confirmation of one of these agreements by the latter is
printed in Derby Charters no. 516, and several
documents relating to this land are entered in the
Rufford Cartulary (Harl. MS. 1063), but the text of
this cartulary is so corrupt that their exact meaning
cannot be recovered. They may be dated *circa* 1190.

Winster

281. Robert f. Col

Grants to William de Mungai, because of the service
which he did to Robert's father and to himself, his

rent (*firma*) of Winster being 6 shillings yearly, to hold of Robert and his heirs by a yearly payment of a red hawk. For this grant William has given to Robert a horse and 40 shillings.

Circa 1170   Derby Charters no. 2620

Scarsdale Wapentake

Brampton

282. Henry f. Ricardi f. Ketel de Brampton

Releases to the priory of St. John the Baptist, Derby, all his right in the *cultura* called Rouland of the fee of Hugh f. Ingerami of Brampton.

Warranty.

Circa 1245   Harl. MS. 1063, f. 120b

The same cartulary (f. 117b) contains an agreement dated 1245–6, by which John f. Walteri f. Ketel demises to Ralf Palmer, for 13 years, a piece of land in Brampton at a yearly rent of 2 shillings.

Duckmanton

283. Hugh f. Leysingi de Dukemantona

Grants to Welbeck abbey all his land between the sheep-fold of the abbey and Alrensik, to hold of him and his heirs in pure and perpetual alms.

Circa 1200   Harl. MS. 3640, f. 65b

284. Hugh f. Leising et heredes sui

Grant to Sured, Hugh's sister, in settlement of a

dispute, 2 bovates with 2 tofts in Duckmanton, to hold of Hugh and his heirs at a yearly rent of 22 pence. If Sured or her heirs wish to sell this land or give it in pledge, they shall offer it first to Hugh and his heirs.

Circa 1220   Ibid. f. 65b

285. Robert f. Goderici de Dukemantona

Grants to the brethren of Solomon's Temple, in perpetual alms, 2 bovates with a toft in Duckmanton. The brethren have received Robert, his heirs, and the soul of William his son *in orationibus et beneficiis que fiunt in omnibus locis ad fraternitatem eorum pertinentibus.* Robert has made this gift in the full chapter of Scarsdale (deanery) at Chesterfield.

Circa 1190   Ibid., f. 71

Langwith

286. Thomas f. Aluerici de Languat

(1) Grants to Welbeck abbey, with his body, all his land in Mosweit and 2 acres at the head of the *cultura* of Wlsicroft, to hold in free, pure, and perpetual alms. The canons have received Thomas into the fraternity of their house.

Circa 1190   Ibid., f. 48b

(2) Grants to the same 6 acres which he held of Hubert of Scarcliffe's fee, to hold in pure and perpetual alms.

Circa 1190   Ibid., f. 48b

Wirksworth Wapentake

Ballidon

287. Ailwin f. Swani, and Robert and Henry *nepotes sui*

Are parties to an agreement by which they grant to
Adam Malet and to whomsoever of his kin he may
choose, the whole right and inheritance which they
have in 4 bovates in Ballidon which they ought to
hold of Richard de Herthul. Adam and his assignee
shall hold this land of them and their heirs at a yearly
rent of 3 pence. For this grant Adam has given 2
marks to Ailwin and his *nepotes.*

Circa 1190   Derby Charters no. 215

Kniveton

288. Robert f. Tholi

(1) Confirms to Sewall de Mungei, in fee and inheritance, the tenement in Winnedon which his father
and Serlo his elder brother held of Robert, to hold of
him and his heirs at a yearly rent of 2 shillings. If
Sewall wishes to settle (*erburgare*) this land, the men
who dwell there shall have free common in wood and
field. Sewall has become Robert's man, and has given
him half a mark for this grant.

Late twelfth century   Derby Charters no. 134

289 Robert f. Tholi

(2) Grants to Humfrey f. Haslac and his heirs the toft
and croft on which Humfrey dwells and 10 acres next

the land of Arnald, Robert's son, towards Arne-
weylotteclough' measured by the perch of 22 feet,
and half the essart of Walter Fot'. To hold of Robert
and his heirs at a yearly rent of half a mark. Robert
reserves the right of granting to Humfrey an exchange
for the half essart of Walter Fot, and will warrant the
whole tenement to Humfrey and his heirs. For this
grant Humfrey has done homage to Robert and given
him a bay horse.

Consent of Robert, Robert's son and heir.

Late twelfth century   Kniveton Leiger, f. 46b

290. Robert f. Tholi

(3) Grants to Matthew f. Humfridi de Knyueton' and
his heirs, for his homage and service, a toft in Kniveton and all the land beneath the essart which Bonde
held, towards the east, at a yearly rent of 2 pence.
For this grant, Matthew has given 5 pence to
Robert.

Warranty.

Sealing clause.

Early thirteenth century   Ibid., f. 47b

291. Robert f. Tholi

(4) Grants to Gilbert f. Ailsi and his heirs for his
homage and service, the meadow lying between
Winnedon' and Askebek' in breadth and between the
meadow of William Basing' and the boundary of

Matthew the clerk *subtus eius tungam* in length, together with 2 acres next the land of Matthew the clerk, at a yearly rent of 6 pence. For this grant, Gilbert has given 20 shillings to Robert.

Circa 1200 Kniveton Leiger, f. 47

292. Dionisia uxor quondam Roberti f. Toly

Releases to Robert her son all her right by reason of dower in a rent of 2 shillings which she received from the land of Elias f. Ricardi. For this grant Robert has given her a mark of silver. She declares herself subject to ecclesiastical jurisdiction, so that the Ordinary may compel her to observe the terms of the grant. Sealing clause.

Circa 1230 Ibid., f. 48b

293. Robert f. Roberti f. Toly

Grants to William de Irton', clerk, a rent of 2 shillings from the 4 bovates in Kniveton which Elias f. Ricardi formerly held, with the homages, reliefs, wardships, and marriages of the successors of Elias. To hold to William and his heirs or assignees at a yearly rent of a sheaf of oats. For this grant William has given 2 marks to Robert.

Warranty.

Sealing clause.

Circa 1230 Ibid., f. 48

294. Robert f. Roberti f. Toly

> Confirms to Elias f. Ricardi f. Orm, for his homage and service, 4 bovates in Kniveton which Richard and his *antecessores* had held. To hold of Robert and his heirs at a yearly rent of 2 shillings.
> Warranty.
> *Circa* 1220   Ibid., f. 47

295. Robert f. Roberti f. Toly

> Grants to John the clerk and his heirs the bovate which Simon held with its toft, croft, and land taken in from the green, and with the toft next that which Ouiet held, to hold of Robert and his heirs at a yearly rent of 12 pence. For this grant John has given 22 shillings to Robert.
> Warranty.
> Sealing clause.
> *Circa* 1220   Ibid.

296. Richard f. Robert f. Toly

> Grants to Matthew f. Humfrey of Kniveton two bovates which Geoffrey the smith held, and the rood which Col held, by way of addition to those bovates. To hold of Richard and his heirs at a yearly rent of 8 pence. For this grant, Matthew has given 30 shillings to Richard.
> Sealing clause.
> *Circa* 1220   Ibid., f. 47b

297. Robert f. Ricardi f. Toly

Grants to Matthew de Knyueton and his heirs or assignees a toft which Henry Bauy formerly held. Sealing clause.

Circa 1230   Kniveton Leiger, f. 47b

298. Roger f. Leuenat de Peuerwik'

Grants to Geoffrey the smith of Ashbourne and his heirs 2 bovates in Kniveton which Suan Gent held, to hold of Roger and his heirs at a yearly rent of 20 pence. For this grant, Geoffrey has given a fine cow with its calf to Roger, and by Geoffrey's advice he has also given 2 shillings to Robert f. Toly to secure his confirmation.

Circa 1200   Ibid., f. 48b

299. As Roger f. Leuenardi de Peu'

Grants to Ralf the clerk f. Gamell' de Peu' and his heirs 2 acres of arable, known by the name of Flat, beneath Ralf's garden, to hold of Roger and his heirs at a yearly rent of a pair of white gloves. For this grant, Ralf has given to Roger *quasdam hesas de Punfredo* before the whole wapentake of Wirksworth *apud Pikedeston*.

Heirs' consent.
Warranty.
Sealing clause.

Circa 1210   Ibid., f. 67b

300. Henry f. Quenild de Knyueton'

Grants to Robert the smith of Ashbourne and his heirs or assignees, for his homage and service, an acre in Kniveton *super longum knollum de Cope*, to hold of Henry and his heirs at a yearly rent of 2 pence.

Warranty.

Sealing clause.

Circa 1230   Ibid., f. 50 b

301. Herbert f. Leuk' de Knyuetona

Grants to Robert f. Roberti Paulyn 3½ acres and 1 rood in Kniveton, of which half an acre lies *super le Flaggihalegh'*, half an acre beyond Esseburnesty, half an acre in Magna Cope *super le Areweylottes*, half an acre *super le Netheregalleforlong'*, *ad le Cloughesheued*, half an acre *super le Shunelebrode*, half an acre *super Hongerforlong'*, half an acre *ad le Ladiwallesiche*, and 1 rood super *le Halwedoles*. To hold of Herbert and his heirs or assignees at a yearly rent of 1 peppercorn. For this grant Robert has given 30 shillings to Herbert.

Warranty.

Sealing clause.

Circa 1260   Ibid., f. 56 b

Wirksworth

302. Hugh f. Osewardi

Grants to Richard f. Willelmi Trusselime a toft, an

ash tree, and half an acre in Wirksworth, to hold of Hugh and his heirs at a yearly rent of 2 shillings.
Warranty.
Sealing clause.

   Circa 1260   **D. & C. Linc. Cartae Decani, f.** 38

Appendix of Charters

I. CALENDAR NO. 6

SCIANT presentes et futuri quod ego Thomas filius Augmundi dedi et concessi et hac presenti carta mea confirmaui. consensu et uoluntate heredum meorum . Willelmo de Netelham pro humagio et seruicio suo unam acram terre ex orientali parte uille de Dunham . et unam aliam acram terre ex occidentali parte uille eiusdem . reddendo mihi et heredibus meis unum denarium pro omni seruitio et omni exactione in uigilia Pasce annuatim. Et sciendum quod altera predictarum acrarum iacet in Hauerhilla . et altera acra iacet in sud parte de Stainbrige . Et hanc donationem warantizabimus ego et heredes mei predicto Willelmo et heredibus suis . contra omnes homines . Hiis testibus . Toraldo de Nouilla . Willelmo de Sudbroc . Humfrido de Riland' . Reginaldo pedeken . Gaufrido de Welleton' . Ricardo de Hainton'.

Thomas son of Augmund, the grantor of this charter, attests three other charters in the same section of the Kirkstead cartulary. In one, he appears as Thomas f. Agmundi, in another, as Thomas f. Acmundi, and in the third, as Thomas f. Aumundi.

II. CALENDAR NO. 13

Sciant omnes presentes et futuri quod ego Robertus filius Agemundi de Scamtun concessi et dedi et hac mea carta

confirmaui deo et ecclesie sancte Marie et monachis de
Kyrkested' in puram et perpetuam elemosinam in territorio
de Scamtun duos seliones extendentes se uersus austrum
et uersus aquilonem . super curtem Gileberti filii Beatrice .
et sciendum quod unam bouatam terre et dimidiam antea
dederam eis cum omnibus pertinenciis suis in pratis et
pasturis et in omnibus aliis aisiamentis insuper et unam
foreram ad Upwell' . et unum selionem in Scadaker de
dimidia acra . in eodem territorio de Scamtun . Hec autem
omnia concessi et dedi eis pro salute mea et omnium pre-
decessorum meorum . et ego et heredes mei warantizabimus predictis monachis omnia predicta contra omnes
homines inperpetuum . Testibus . Gileberto filio Thome .
Andrea clerico . Thoma auunculo eius Roberto Huripel .
Roberto homine abbatis . Roberto Martel . Hugone de
Badhou . Rainaldo de Haddecliue . Waltero Cole. Seal as
described in Calendar.

This grant was confirmed by Richard f. Roberti f. Agenumdi
de Scamton' (Cott. Vesp. E xviii, f. 188). Anketin f. Ricardi de
Scamton' quitclaims to the monks of Kirkstead all the land which
he held in Scampton of them and the monks of Norwich, and all
the land which Robert f. Agmundi gave them. Anketin will hold
of the monks of Kirkstead whatever he may acquire of the remaining two bovates which Robert's heirs hold, for the service by which
Robert and his heirs held (ibid.).

III. CALENDAR NO. 24

Sciant omnes presentes et futuri . quod ego Radulfus filius
Alani filii Besi de Ulesbi . concessi et dedi et presenti

carta confirmaui . deo et ecclesie et monachis sancte Marie
de Kyrkested' . in puram et perpetuam elemosinam duas
acras terre arabilis in teritorio [*sic*] de Ulesbi . ad tenendum
de me et heredibus meis . et iacent in hiis locis . scilicet
tres seliones super Filintwang proximo terre eorundem
monachorum . et super Gumpedailam unum selionem et
extendit se super foreram Willelmi filii Ketelli et i selionem
in Satheraiwag . in terras eorundem monachorum . et in
Brakendala i selionem iuxta terram eorundem monachorum
et ex sut parte de Driuedal' dimidiam acram . Totas predictas terras dedi predictis monachis pro duabus acris siue
plus siue minus fuerit in eis . et ego et heredes mei warantizabimus et acquietabimus uersus omnes homines de omnibus rebus ad opus predictorum monachorum . predictas
terras . ut habeant et teneant eas libere et quiete ab omni
seculari seruicio . et consuetudine . et exactione in perpetuam elemosinam . Testibus Henrico capellano Baldrico
de Grendal' . Roberto Martel . Henrico de Wdehale .
Gaufrido de Faraford.

IV. CALENDAR NO. 32

Omnibus sancte ecclesie filiis presentibus et futuris Tori
carpentarius et Umfridus clericus et Walterus Lumbardus
et Robertus de Apulia et Walterus filius Godrici et Gille-
bertus Skerewind salutem . Sciatis nos concessisse et
dedisse in elemosinam deo et ecclesie sancte Marie de
Kirkesteda et monachis eiusdem loci quicquid unquam
iuris habuimus uel clamauimus in terra illa que iacet inter

abbatiam monachorum ipsorum et Stikeswald et uadit in latum a trencato monachorum usque ad uiam que ducit ad Widmam et in longum a molendino de Sinker quod est monachorum usque ad ipsam aquam Widme et ut totam hanc terram teneant libere et quiete ab omni seculari seruitio et consuetudine et exactione et omni reclamatione nostri uel heredum nostrorum Et hoc totum fecimus eis pro salute nostra et animarum nostrarum et omnium antecessorum nostrorum et ut participes simus omnium bonorum que fiunt uel facienda sunt in domo de Kirk' in perpetuum . Insuper et per propriam uoluntatem nostram super sacramenta iurauimus hec omnia firmiter tenere et quod nunquam queremus illis nec per nos ipsos nec per alium aliquam occasionem uel disturbationem unde sint perdentes aliquid uel in aliquo disturbati de predicta terra . Testibus . Roberto Calf . Roberto de Hattuna . Gilleberto Norrisco Waltero de Bart' Henrico de Leirtuna.

V. CALENDAR NO. 33

Willelmus filius Ketelli et Willelmus filius Alani nepos eius omnibus sancte ecclesie filiis presentibus et futuris salutem Sciatis nos concessisse et dedisse et hac carta nostra confirmasse deo et ecclesie sancte Marie de Kirk' et monachis eiusdem loci in perpetuam elemosinam quicquid pertinet ad ius nostrum a fossato quod uadit a trencato grangie abbatie uersus aquilonem usque ad publicam uiam que uadit uersus Witmam et ab ipso fossato quicquid est inter predictam uiam et curtem grangie uersus orientem usque ad uadum subtus molendinum de Sinker ut predicti monachi habeant et teneant predicta libere et quiete ad faciendum inde quicquid uoluerint Testibus magistro Gilleberto Rundel Symone de Hornecast' Edric brun Willelmo filio Symonis Ragam' filio Goscelini Martino Furmage Johanne Neth.

VI. CALENDAR NO. 35

Notum sit omnibus presentibus et futuris quod ego Rei-gotus filius Wilgirb de Drextorp . consessi et presenti carta confirmaui . deo et ecclesie sancte Marie de Kyrkest' et monachis eiusdem loci . in puram et perpetuam elemo-sinam . dimidiam acram terre arabilis in campis de Drex-torp prope Onkelbusker . et iacet inter terram Ricardi Waifhin et terram Roberti le ueel . et extendit se super terram Roberti le paumer uersus orientem . et uersus occidentem super terram Henrici le duck . cum alio selione in campis de Langt' super Spelhoufurlang . et iacet inter terram Johannis filii decani . et terram Warini filii Wlmari . et se extendit uersus le est a forera Hugonis de Dalbi super le grenegate . Omnia predicta habebunt predicti monachi . et tenebunt . libere et quiete ab omni seculari seruicio et consuetudine . et exactione . sicut ulla elemosina . melius et liberius teneri potest . cum communi pastura ad tan-tumdem terre pertinete [*sic*] . et ego et heredes mei warantizabimus eis omnia predicta contra omnes homines inperpetuum . Testibus Henrico capellano de Langet' Radulfo de Grend' Randulfo de Dalbi . Matheo fratre eius . Simone filio Franc' . Roberto filio Gaufridi Eudone.

VII. CALENDAR NO. 36

Sciant omnes qui legunt uel audiunt hoc scriptum quod
ego Eilricus de Sazstorp . concessi et dedi et hac presenti
carta confirmaui pro salute anime mee et omnium antecessorum meorum . deo et ecclesie et monachis sancte
Marie de Kyrk' in puram et perpetuam elemosinam iios
seliones in campis de Langeton' . quos habui in Coldicwra
pro una acra siue plus siue minus fuerit in eis . et communem pasturam in eisdem campis quantum pertinet ad tan-
tumdem terre et ego et heredes mei warantizabimus et
acquietabimus predictis monachis omnia predicta contra
omnes homines . ut monachi habeant et teneant omnia
libere et quiete . sine omni seculari seruicio . et consuetudine . et exactione . in perpetuam elemosinam . Testibus
Henrico capellano . Reinaldo Pilat . Johanne de Halton' .
Simone de Langeton' . Daniel filius [*sic*] Toruerth'.

VIII. CALENDAR NO. 37

Sciant presentes et futuri quod ego Haldanus filius Wluieti
de Askeby concessi et dedi et hac mea carta confirmaui deo
et ecclesie beate Marie de Kyrkest' et monachis eiusdem
loci unam perticatam prati in territorio de Askeby . uideli-
cet in sud parte de Benedal' et iacet inter pratum ipsorum
monachorum ex utraque parte . ut habeant et teneant
predictum pratum in liberam et puram et perpetuam
elemosinam cum omnibus pertinentiis suis . Ita quod nec
ego uel heredes mei aliquam calumpnian in predicto prato
uendicare uel habere poterimus . Et ego Haldanus et

heredes mei warantizabimus predictum pratum ad opus predictorum monachorum et de omni seculari seruitio consuetudine et exactione acquietabimus contra omnes homines inperpetuum . Hiis testibus . Ricardo decano de Hornecast' . etc.

The 'decanus de Hornecast' is the rural dean of Horncastle wapentake.

IX. CALENDAR NO. 38

Sciant presentes et futuri quod ego Hugo filius Brunneys de Askeby concessi et dedi et presenti carta confirmaui deo et monachis sancte Marie de Kirkest' . in puram et perpetuam elemosinam in campis de Askeby ex west parte eiusdem uille totum selionem quem habui ex nord parte uie de Linc' . quantum se habet in latum . scilicet ii perticatas et quantum idem selio extendit se in longum iuxta terram propriam monachorum cum communi pastura quantum pertinet ad tantumdem terre in predictis campis Et ego et heredes mei warantizabimus et acquietabimus omnia predicta uersus omnes homines ut ipsi monachi habeant et teneant ea libere et quiete sine omni seculari seruitio et consuetudine et exactione in perpetuam elemosinam . Testibus . Willelmo capellano . Walone . Rogero filio Normanni . Henrico de Wdehall'.

X. CALENDAR NO. 42

Sciant omnes presentes et futuri quod ego Robertus filius Thori de Cuninghesbi concessi et dedi et presenti carta confirmaui deo et ecclesie sancte Marie de Kirkested' et monachis eiusdem loci in puram et perpetuam elemosinam donationem Henrici filii Walteri de Cuningesbi . scilicet totam medietatem culture que est inter Fermerakebusc et terram Nicholai filii Siuerd et pratum in Westmerholm et communem pasturam et cetera sicut carta predicti Henrici quam monachi habent testatur . Et hec omnia warantizabimus eis ego et heredes mei contra omnes homines in perpetuum . Testibus Hugone capellano de Cuningesbi . Roberto homine abbatis . A. Martel.

XI. CALENDAR NO. 44

Omnibus sancte ecclesie filiis presentibus et futuris . Willelmus gener Ulf de Cunighesbi salutem Sciatis me per concessionem et bonam uoluntatem Matildis sponse mee et heredum meorum concessisse et dedisse et hac mea carta in feodo firmam et perpetuam elemosinam confirmasse deo et ecclesie sancte Marie de Kirk' et monachis eiusdem loci pro salute animarum nostrarum unam piscariam in Widma que uocatur Aldehida quam ipsi monachi antea tenuerunt de predicto Ulf socero meo et quam ipse Ulf eis antea similiter in elemosinam concesserat . ut ipsi monachi habeant et teneant ipsam piscariam libere et quiete . sicut unquam elemosina que in feudo firma tenetur liberius et quietius teneri potest pro reddendo nobis inde annuatim xii denarios. scilicet iii ad festum Botulfi . et iii ad festum sancti Michaelis et iii ad Natale domini et iii ad Pasca uel vi sticcas anguillarum ad festum sancti Martini pro omni seruitio et consuetudine et exactione . Et ego et heredes mei

warantizabimus et de nostro alio tenemento acquietabimus
ad opus ipsorum monachorum de omnibus aliis rebus contra omnes homines in perpetuum . Et hoc totum affidaui
ego Willelmus manu mea in manu Nicholai Bec fideliter
tenendum sine omni malo ingenio inperpetuum . Testibus
Nicholao Bec Johanne clerico de Wdehalla Henrico filio
Alani Johanne de Timmelbi Gaufrido de Langet'.

XII. CALENDAR NO. 45

Notum sit omnibus presentibus et futuris quod ego Ricardus filius Sigwardi de Cunighesbi . concessi et dedi et
presenti carta confirmaui deo et ecclesie sancte Marie et
monachis de Kyrkested' totam partem meam illius piscarie
in Widma que uocatur Holdehihe scilicet quartam partem .
habendam et tenendam cum pertinentiis suis in perpetuam
elemosinam . reddendo inde annuatim pro omnibus rebus
et seruitiis tres denarios . scilicet tres obolos ad Natale . et
tres obolos . ad Pascha. Et ego et heredes mei warantizabimus predictis monachis totam predictam quartam partem
predicte piscarie . Testibus . Osberto de Cunighesbi . Roberto homine abbatis . Gilleberto filio Roberti . Willelmo
fratre eius . Rogero filio Godrici . Waltero Lirth . Waltero
filio Roberti.

XIII. CALENDAR NO. 47

Notum sit omnibus presentibus et futuris quod ego Adelsi
de Kyrkeby . concessi et quietum clamaui deo et ecclesie
sancte Marie et monachis de Kyrkested' totum jus et
clamium quod umquam habui uel habere potui uersus eos

de clausis suis apud molendinum de Beyna . ut habeant et teneant ipsa clausa tam in ortis quam in edificiis libera et quieta de me et heredibus meis in perpetuam elemosinam . Et hoc feci eis pro salute anime mee . et heredum meorum Hiis testibus . Roberto de Scrembi . Petro persona de Ructon' . Johanne fratre eius . Henrico de Langetona . Roberto Martel de Kanewic . Huberto filio Warini . Waltero Cole.

XIV. CALENDAR NO. 49

Omnibus sancte ecclesie filiis presentibus et futuris Gaufridus filius Alberici de Mart' salutem . Sciatis me concessisse et dedisse et hac mea carta confirmasse deo et ecclesie sancte Marie de Kirk' et monachis eiusdem loci in puram et perpetuam elemosinam totum illud pratum quod uocatur Dunesholm . habendum et tenendum libere et quiete sine omni seculari seruitio et consuetudine et omni exactione . et hanc donationem warantizabo eis contra omnes homines et hoc totum affidaui in manu Alani de Mart' . et hoc feci per bonam uoluntatem et concessionem Acke filii Grimkel . qui ipsum pratum tenuit Et ego Acke concedo predictis monachis ipsum pratum quantum ad me et heredes pertinet in puram et perpetuam elemosinam . et warantizabo illud et acquietabo contra omnes homines in perpetuum et hoc totum affidaui firmiter et fideliter tenendum absque omni malo ingenio in manu Ketelli le matzun . Testibus Henrico sacerdote de Askebi . Ricardo de Bard' . Johanne clerico de Wdehall' . Alano de Mart' . Roberto Calf.

XV. CALENDAR NO. 55

Notum sit omnibus sancte dei ecclesie filiis tam presentibus quam futuris quod ego Willelmus filius Grimchelli concessi et dedi ecclesie sancte Marie de Kirk' et monachis ibidem deo seruientibus lx acras terre de mea propria hereditate in campis Strat' . in perpetuam elemosinam . scilicet illam terram que ultra quicsand et si quid ibi defuerit perficiam eis in occidentali parte uie de Eilouagate et eandem uiam quia minus stricta erat amplificabo de mea propria terra et preter hec communem pasturam per totos campos predictos pro salute anime mee et patris mei et omnium parentum meorum et pratum inter Blacwell' et Eilougata in australi parte riuuli Et Symon et Robertus filii Aki cognati mei dederunt ecclesie predicte xvi acras super Holm in elemosinam et predictus Symon dedit ex sua parte xv acras in campis predictis et unam partem prati dedit Symon ecclesie predicte quod pratum iacet iuxta pratum quod dominus Willelmus dedit . et Hugo clericus dedit iiiior acras ecclesie predicte in elemosinam . Et Symon et Robertus predicti dederunt communem pasturam prefate ecclesie per campos predictos et ego Willelmus filius Grimkelli confirmo totam donationem Symonis et Roberti et Hugonis . His testibus Johanne abbate de Barden' Philippo de Edlingtuna Willelmo filio Haconis Maci de Curci Hugone Malet.

This gift was confirmed by R de Curci, whose charter is entered on the same folio of the Kirkstead cartulary:

R. de Curci et A sponsa sua A dei gratia Linc' episcopo totique capitulo sancte Marie Linc' salutem Sciatis Willelmum de Stret' filium Grimkel concessisse et dedisse ecclesie sancte Marie de Kirk' et monachis ibidem deo seruientibus in nostra presentia lx acras de propria hereditate quam tenet de nobis in Stret' scilicet illam terram que ultra quicsand et si quid ibi defuerit implebitur eis ab occidente de Allofgata et eandem uiam quia minus stricta est amplificabit de sua propria terra in feudo et perpetua elemosina . et preter hec communem pasturam terre sue . quam concessionem et donationem nos cupientes participes fieri beneficiorum tante congregationis ipso Willelmo suppliciter petente pro salute anime nostre concedendo et donando quia de propria hereditate nostra est donationem confirmamus Testes Maci de Curci Hugo Maleth Symon de Stret' Adam filius Alani filii Glaii.

XVI. CALENDAR NO. 65

Notum sit omnibus sancte ecclesie filiis presentibus et futuris quod ego Eustacius de Cathebi et heredes mei concedimus et damus deo et ecclesie sancte Marie de Kirkestede et monachis eius [*sic*] loci totam terram plenarie in puram et perpetuam elemosinam quam Jaalf de Sudtorp teneuit [*sic*] de Swano de Cathebi ab australi parte uie que uadit aput Ludam Hanc terram damus eis libere et quiete ab omni seculari seruitio et consuetudine et omni exactione et acquietabimus illam eis contra omnes homines de omnibus rebus Sed et hoc sciendum est quod ego et frater meus et heredes nostri clamamus monachis quietum totum ius et calumniam quam habuimus in terra Willelmi Trig de Saxedale et cum eis stabimus contra omnes homines quicunque mouebit illis calumpniam siue querelam de terra illa scilicet pro posse nostrum [*sic*] fideliter per expensas monachorum et hoc affidauit [*sic*] tenendum in manu Walteri uicecomitis . Teste domino Hugone abbate de Wardune et Symone cellarario Nigello de Couentre;

The fact that Swan 'de Cathebi' was father of Eustace, the grantor of this charter, appears from the following document, entered on the same folio of the cartulary:

Uniuersis sancte matris ecclesie filiis tam presentibus quam futuris Alanus de Baiocis salutem . Sciatis quod Eustacius filius Swani de Catebi homo meus concessit et dedit abbatie de Kirkestede unam culturam in campis de Catebi que uocatur Cheigelwang scilicet . ix . acras in puram et perpetuam elemosinam liberam et quietam ab omni terreno seruicio siue dono cum communi pastura terre sue Hanc donationem fecit per concessum heredum suorum fide interposita quod stabilis ista donatio permanebit et ut hec elemosina firmiter stet ego hanc concessi et sigillo contra omnes calumpnias confirmaui Huius rei testes sunt Radulfus abbas de Parco . Walterus abbas de Bardeneia Gualo abbas de Sancto Laurencio.

XVII. CALENDAR NO. 176

Omnibus sancte ecclesie filiis presentibus et futuris Turoldus Welletun' salutem Sciatis me per bonam uoluntatem et

consilium Alberede mee sponse et Walteri filii mei et here-
dis concessisse et dedisse et hac mea carta confirmasse deo
et ecclesie sancte Marie de Kirkestede et monachis eiusdem
loci in puram et perpetuam elemosinam quicquid est de
feudo meo per has diuisas scilicet quatuor percatas in
latum in quarantenis de Spelhou et iiiior percatas in latum
ab occidentali parte de Rouhewell' . Preterea dedi eis iiii
percatas in latum ad australem partem de Eggedale et
quicquid est de feudo meo a Spelhou sicut Eggedale uadit
usque ad Routhewell' [*sic*] ut habeant et teneant omnia
honorifice libere et quiete sine omni seculari seruitio et
consuetudine et omni exactione . et hoc ita eis warantizan-
dum et adquietandum de omnibus rebus et seruitiis erga
omnes homines inperpetuum affidauimus ego Thuroldus et
Walterus filius meus et heres in manu Helye sacerdotis de
Gait' . Testibus . eodem sacerdote . Joze de Gait' . Alano
palmario.

XVIII. CALENDAR NO. 181

Omnibus sancte ecclesie filiis presentibus et futuris Robertus filius Agemundi de Cotes . salutem . Sciatis me concessisse et dedisse et hac mea carta confirmasse deo et
ecclesie sancte Marie de Kirk' et monachis eiusdem loci in
puram et perpetuam elemosinam . iij . perticatas terre in
latum ex sud parte de Engedale inter terram Thoraldi et
terram que fuit Willelmi Trig . libere et quiete ab omni
seculari seruitio et consuetudine et exactione . Et ego et
heredes mei warantizabimus . et acquitabimus terram illam

de omnibus rebus et seruitiis erga omnes homines . et hoc totum feci eis per concessionem Johannis generi mei ita quod ipse Johannes confirmauit hanc donationem meam per appositionem sigilli sui . Testibus . Helia sacerdote de Gait' . Roberto de Biscopt' persona . magistro Geruesio [*sic*] de Grimkeltorp . W de Fulletebi.

XIX. CALENDAR NO. 185

Notum sit omnibus presentibus et futuris quod ego Symon filius Stainbid de Sunethorp dedi et concessisse et hac presenti carta mea confirmaui deo et sancte Marie de Kirkested' . et monachis ibidem deo seruientibus in puram et perpetuam elemosinam unum selionem in campis de Sunethorp . scilicet ex orientali parte curie eorundem monachorum qui iacet inter culturam que fuit Hugonis de Merula . et culturam que fuit Gregorii de Sunethorp . et se extendit a porta predicte curie . usque ad diuisam de Snelleslund . Et ego et heredes mei warantizabimus predictis monachis predictum selionem . et acquietabimus de omnibus rebus contra omnes homines . Hiis . testibus . Heltone de Snelleslund Willelmo fratre suo Thoma fratre persone . Stephano filio persone Suain Haribrun Roberto . fabro Gilberto clerico et ceteris.

XX. CALENDAR NO. 199

Omnibus sancte ecclesie filiis presentibus et futuris Thomas filius Suani salutem Sciatis me concessisse et dedisse . et hac mea carta confirmasse . deo et ecclesie sancte Marie de

Kirkestede et monachis eiusdem loci in elemosinam . unam
acram terre arabilis in campis de Branzton' . ad occidenta-
lem partem uille de feodo Osberti de Hanewrd' . quam ego
aliquando calumpniatus fueram . et dimidiam acram terre
in eisdem campis de feodo Fulqui . del Alnei . uersus
Drepwel . libere et quiete de omni seculari seruitio et consuetudine . et omni exactione . pro salute mea et omnium
antecessorum meorum . Testibus . Simone de Blankeneia
Norman filio Baldewini de Bocland' . Georgio Grim .
Amfredo filio Johannis de Risctun' . Iuone de Rowell' .
Reinaldo filio Hugonis.

XXI. CALENDAR NO. 200

Sciant presentes et futuri quod ego Rogerus filius Haconis
de Haneword' dedi et concessi et hac presenti carta mea
confirmaui . Ricardo filio meo tres bouatas terre arabilis in
territorio de Haneword' cum duobus toftis et edificiis que
tenebat Orgarus Lincoln' in Haneword' . et unam boutam
terre quam Robertus frater meus tenet in uita sua quam
ipse Ricardus post obitum predicti Roberti accipiet . cum
omnibus pertinenciis infra uillam et extra . scilicet . in
pratis in pascuis . in campis et boscis et mariscis . et in
omnibus locis predictis terre et tofto [*sic*] pertinentibus .
Tenend*um* et habend*um* libere et quiete . integre . pacifice .
sine retinemento sibi et heredibus suis uel assignatis uel
cuicunque dare uel assignare uel uendere uoluerit et
quando inperpetuum . reddendo inde annuatim x solidos
argenti . Philippo de Marton' uel suis heredibus ad iiii

terminos scilicet . ad Pascha ii solidos et dimidium . ad festum sancti Johannis baptiste tantum . et ad festum sancti Michaelis tantum . et ad Natale domini tantum . pro omnibus seruiciis excepto seruicio domini regis et illud faciet prout proportat carta Wlrici'[1] . Et ut hec mea donacio etc.

XXII. CALENDAR NO. 201

Uniuersis sancte matris ecclesie filiis hanc cartam visuris vel audituris Deulewardus filius Arketil de Scaup' salutem Sciatis me concessisse dedisse et presenti carta mea confirmasse deo et ecclesie beati Petri apostoli de Thurgartona et canonicis ibidem deo seruientibus dimidiam acram terre arabilis et quatuor reones in territorio de Scaup' . scilicet . unam rodam inter selionem dictorum canonicorum in Wrothedal . et selionem Johannis Palmer' . et unam rodam et quatuor reones que abuttat [*sic*] super foreram de Wrothdal . scilicet . inter dictos canonicos . et Rogerum Pudel . tenendum et habendum dictis canonicis in liberam puram et perpetuam elemosinam sicut aliqua elemosina liberius potest dari vel teneri . Et ego Deulewardus et heredes mei dictam dimidiam acram terre et quatuor reones dictis canonicis warantizabimus contra omnes homines in

[1] These words are explained by a charter of Walter de Aincurt (Thurgarton Cartulary folio 97b) confirming to 'Wlric' de Haneword' four bovates which his father had held, and two 'mansiones' which Ofram and Hachun had held. This charter states that Wulfric is only to do service to the King as a certain Herveius does, and need not attend the wapentake court nor pleas of the crown. The Hachun of this charter, which may be dated *circa* 1160, is probably identical with Hacon, father of the grantor of the present document.

perpetuum . pro salute anime mee et omnium antecessorum et successorum meorum . et ut hec mea etc.

XXIII. CALENDAR NO. 202

Sciant omnes tam presentes quam futuri quod ego Deuleward' filius Arkel de Scaup' consilio et consensu uxoris me et heredum meorum dedi et concessi et hac carta mea confirmaui Heruico le neucomen de Scaup' et heredibus suis uel cuicunque assignare uoluerit dimidiam acram terre arabilis in territorio de Scaup' et de Kirkeby iacentem ex norparte uille de Kirkeby super Engdikfurlong iuxta terram Walteri filii Moysant' Tenendum et habendum libere et quiete integre et pacifice in feodo et hereditate inperpetuum de me et de heredibus meis sine impedimento alicuius reddendo inde annuatim mihi et heredibus meis unum obolum ad pascha pro omni seruicio et consuetudine et exaccione Ego uero Deuleward' et heredes mei warantizabimus acquietabimus et defendemus predictam terram predicto Heruico et heredibus suis uel cuicumque assignare uoluerit propter predictam firmam contra omnes homines qui possunt uiuere et mori Et ut hec confirmacio etc.

XXIV. CALENDAR NO. 203

Sciant omnes presentes et futuri quod ego Galfridus filius Herewardi de Scaup' dedi et concessi et hac mea presenti carta confirmaui Waltero clerico filio meo et heredibus uel assignatis suis duas acras terre arabilis cum pertinenciis in territorio de Scaup' . scilicet . ex north parte uille dimidiam acram terre super Musethornfurlong' et dimidiam acram super Littelpitteshil et ex south parte uille dimidiam acram terre ultra Gildusgate et dimidiam acram in Ety . iacentem inter terram Alexandri filii Bele et terram Jordani de Esseby Habend' et tenend' in feodo et hereditate libere et quiete pacifice et integre . reddendo inde annuatim mihi et heredibus meis unum obolum ad Natale domini . pro omni seruicio et consuetudine et exaccione Et ego Galfridus et heredes mei warantizabimus et defendemus et acquietabimus totum prenominatum tenementum predicto Waltero filio meo et heredibus suis uel cui assignare uoluerit et heredibus illius cui assignauerit contra omnes homines inperpetuum pro predicto seruicio Hiis testibus Roberto simplici decano etc.

XXV. CALENDAR NO. 204

Uniuersis presens scriptum uisuris uel audituris Rogerus filius Wluiue de Kirkeby salutem . Nouerit uniuersitas uestra me concessisse et quietumclamasse de me et omnibus meis inperpetuum Willelmo priori et conuentui de Thurgartona et eorum successoribus totum ius et clamium quodcunque habui uel habeo uel uendicare potero in tribus bouatis et dimidia prati cum pertinenciis in prato de Kirkeby et de Scaup' . iacentibus ubique inter pratum fratrum templariorum de Bruera extra Riskefen . quas quidem bouatas et dimidiam dictis fratribus concessi et per cirograffum dimisi usque ad terminum xii annorum

termino incipiente ad Pascha anno . regni regis . Henrici
filii regis Johannis . xxmo vito . Insuper obligaui me ipsum
dictis priori et conuentui et eorum successoribus per
omnia que per cartam suam mihi contulerunt ad waranti-
zandum eisdem totum dictum pratum coram iusticiis
domini regis simul cum omnibus terris quas de dono meo
habent per cartam in territorio de Kirkeby et de Scaup' .
et in omnibus redditibus et tenementis eisdem a me collatis.
Et ut hec etc.

XXVI. CALENDAR NO. 205

Uniuersis sancte matris ecclesie filiis Rogerus filius Swayn
de Blaunkeney salutem . Nouerit uniuersitas vestra me
dedisse et hac mea carta confirmasse deo et ecclesie sancte
Crucis de Kirkeby totum pratum quod est habui in mersco
[sic] quod est inter Kirkeby et Scaup' . scilicet . unam per-
catam et dimidiam in latum et in longum a via usque ad
cursum aque . in liberam . puram . et perpetuam elemosinam Ita tamen quod Robertus decanus tenebit illud de
predicta ecclesia reddendo per annum unum obolum ad
festum sancti Botulphi ad lumen seruiendum pro omni
seruicio Et sciendum est quod predictus Robertus bene
poterit dare totum predictum tenementum cuicunque
voluerit tenendum in feodo et hereditate de predicta
ecclesia per predictum seruicium Et ego et heredes mei
warantizabimus predictum tenementum predicte ecclesie
et predicto Roberto et cuicunque idem Robertus illud
dederit et heredibus illius cui illud dederit contra omnes

homines in omnibus inperpetuum Hiis testibus Augustinus capellanus de Scaupewic etc.

XXVII. CALENDAR NO. 206

Sciant presentes et futuri quod ego Simon capellanus filius Willelmi filii Lundi de Scaup' dedi concessi et quietum clamaui Amabilie sorori mee et Roberto uiro suo de Roueston' et eorum heredibus uel assignatis eorum totum ius et clamium quod habui uel habere potui in uno dimidio tofto cum dimidio crofto uersus orientem pertinente ad illud toftum cuius alteram partem Thomas filius Heruici tenuit de me . et in una acra terre iacente in territorio de Scaup' et de Kirkeby . scilicet . una dimidia acra iacet supra Askelhil iuxta terram canonicorum de Thurg' ex australi parte . et una perticata terre iuxta terram Ade filii Hugonis . ex boreali parte buttans super uiam de Diggeby et una perticata terre ad Lingeheuedland' iuxta terram fratrum de Catteley ex orientali parte cum seruicio duorum et oboli . quos Thomas filius Heruici mihi reddere consueuit pro altera medietate predicti tofti et crofti . Tenendum et habendum predicte Amabilie sorori mee et predicto Roberto et heredibus eorum uel assignatis eorum libere quiete pacifice et hereditarie . reddendo inde annuatim fabrice ecclesie beati Petri de Thurg' . iiii . denarios ad festum apostolorum Petri et Pauli . et unum denarium ad ceram ecclesie sancti Andree de Scaup' pro eadem terra ad Pascha pro omni seruicio consuetudine et demanda . Et ut hec etc.

Ibid. Simon grants to Amabilia a toft with a croft and easements which William formerly held of the prior and convent of Thurgarton and one acre in Scopwick and Kirkby Green.

XXVIII. CALENDAR NO. 269

Notum sit tam presentibus quam futuris quod ego Hugo filius Alredi de Carleton' concessi et dedi et hac presenti carta confirmaui deo et beato Petro de Thurgarton' et canonicis ibidem deo seruientibus toftam et croftam que fuerunt Auki et unam bouatam terre quam Rogerus clericus tenuit in Carleton' in puram et perpetuam elemosinam cum communi pastura et cum omnibus aisiamentis terre mee eiusdem uille solutas liberas et quietas ab omni seculari seruicio et exaccione sicut elemosina liberius potest dari Et hanc donacionem meam acquietabunt heredes mei ab omni seruicio et warantizabunt predictis canonicis contra omnes homines inperpetuum Hiis testibus etc.

This charter was confirmed by Robert filius Hugonis filii Aldredi de Carletona and by William filius Hugonis filii Aldredi de Carletona (same folio). The texts are virtually identical with the original grant.

XXIX. CALENDAR NO. 276

Sciant presentes et futuri quod ego Rogerus filius Suani assensu uxoris mee et heredum meorum dedi et concessi et hac carta mea confirmaui deo et canonicis ecclesie beati Petri de Thurgarton' toftam unam in Thurgarton' quam scilicet Agnes filia Manfridi tenet de prenominatis canonicis et unam bouatam terre in campis eiusdem uille cum

omnibus pertinenciis suis in puram et perpetuam elemosinam pro anima mea et uxoris mee et omnium parentum
meorum Hiis testibus Henrico capellano . Nicholao diacono .
Willelmo clerico de Thorp magistro Alexandro Ricardo
coco Manfrido Roberto filio eius Willelmo le bel Ranulpho
filio eius Roberto filio Rogeri Roberto filio eius Henrico
filio Gilberti Willelmo fratre eius   Rogero   Georgio.

General Index

THIS is a small book and it might be felt that an index is unnecessary, but curiously enough, while doing what is not perhaps a very systematic index, it has seemed to me that the value of this collection becomes much more evident. The pride in ancestry which makes grantors, however humble, set out their grandparents' and parents' names and often those of their wives as well, makes it much more difficult to do a good index. Should one enter a man's name under his own name, his father's, his grand-father's, or under the village where he lived or the religious house to which he was making a gift? The small, sometimes extremely small, pieces of land given or sold, make it difficult to decide whether some villages were over-full of inhabitants and whether the price of land was high or low. The occasional hint that life was hard since a man may sell land in his necessity or his great necessity is no more than a hint, perhaps even not that, for some men will never prosper and others cannot seem to help prospering. There was nothing static about the rural society in the Danelaw and I am reminded of my husband's strong assurance that the Anglo-Saxon Society was no more static than the post-Conquest society, that men could rise from peasant to thegnly rank and win seat and service in the king's hall. See *Collected Papers* 'The Thriving of the Anglo-Saxon Ceorl', pp. 304–93.

Subjects are entered with lower case initial letters. Names of people and places with capitals.

A: *see* Eau, the Great

Acke, Acche: *see* Martin by Horn-castle; Skidbrook; Wraggoe

acre:
  2 selions reckoned as 1, 36
  an acre and a quarter with appurtenant pasture, 39

Adam s. of Robert s. of Molée: grants land to Thoui his brother, 116

Adelsi:
  s. of Bern, the fee of, 50
  held of Robert Marmiun's fee, 51
  his *nepos*: *see* Calf, Robert

affidatio in manu:
  of chaplain, 46, 50, 51

of priest, 163, 176, App. XVII, 193
of clerk, 165
of grantee's man, 43
of another grantor, 53, 54
of Walter the sheriff, 65
of squire, 78
of third party, 44, 49, 53, 126
to observe agreement, 183
to warrant the gift, 72
of man whose seal appended to document, 261
of monk, 256

Agge: *see* Boothby; Navenby

Agmund; Agemund; Augmund; Aumund; Acmund: *see* Cotes; Dunholme; Scampton

Index

Dumping:

Ketell, Getell; grants to the church of St. Mary of Lincoln 5 a. of land with Odo his son who shall hold the land at a yearly rent of 12*d.*, 93

Rannulf s. of Getell, grants to Andrew s. of Odo Galle all his land between that of John s. of Odo Dumping on the west and that of Osbert, the parson's son and the graveyard of All Saints, Saltfleetby on the east for a yearly rent of 4*d.*, 114

Dunesholm, meadow in Martin by Horncastle called, 49

Dunholme, Lincs. (Dunham), 6–11

Brictiua of, *alias* widow of Tholard, *alias* Thorald grants to William de Croymar half a bovate of her marriage portion at a yearly rent of a pair of gloves and a lb. of cummin, 7

Brictiua widow of Tholard of, confirms to Kirkstead the gift which her husband and afterwards William de Croymare made to that house, 8

Richard s. of Thorald Cok of, grants to Kirkstead a bovate in, 9

Richard s. of Thorald Cok of, quitclaims to Kirkstead his father's land in, which Martin of Dunholme formerly held, 10

Thomas s. of Thorald Cok of, quitclaims to the same half a bovate and one acre in augmentation, 11

Thomas s. of Agmund of, grants to William of Nettleham 1 a. to east and 1 a. to west of the village for a yearly rent of 1*d.*, 6

Eakring, Notts.:

Gilbert of Skegby alias Gilbert s. of Wulsi s. of Wulf of, agrees with the monks of Rufford granting them 10 a. which his father held of William de Albani in, at a rent of 8*d.* yearly for his life only, 259

Robert s. of Scakel and Herbert his brother grant to Rufford abbey 5 a. and 1 rood in, and quitclaim a bovate in Rufford which Ougrim their uncle held and Robert his son gave in alms when he became a monk, 256

William s. of Robert s. of Arkill of, confirms to the same the a. his father gave and adds another of his own gift, 258

Wlsi s. of Wlf of, surrenders to the same 3 a. he holds of them. His son Godguin to be kept in Rufford until of full age to become, if he wishes, a lay brother; if not, the monks to keep the land, 257

Eau, the Great: see A, 170

Edenham, Lincs.:

Hugh s. of Gilla of, granted to Vaudey abbey 9 a. and 1 rood of arable and meadow, in, 192

Edith, Hedus, Edusa, Edus, and on seal Edit, 178 n.: *see* Welton le Wold

Edlington:

John of, yearly rent of 1 lb. of cummin for 4 of his 8 a. granted to Kirkstead abbey by Robert Calf, 50

Philip of, witn., App. XV

Edric brun, witn., App. V. *see* Grimoldby

Eilric: *see* Ailric

[1] ? orchards and hedges.

PRINTED IN GREAT BRITAIN
AT THE UNIVERSITY PRESS, OXFORD
BY VIVIAN RIDLER
PRINTER TO THE UNIVERSITY